A Visual Guide to Scales for Tenor Banjo in GDAE

Benjamin M. Taylor

Contents

Introduction 4
    The Aims of This Book 4
    Why Learn to Play Scales? 4
    How to Use This Book 4
    Using Scale Diagrams to Construct Exercises 5
    Author's Notes on this Edition 5
Root note: C 7
    C Aeolian 7
    C Algerian 7
    C Arabic 7
    C Bebop Dominant 7
    C Bebop Major 7
    C Bebop Minor 7
    C Chinese 7
    C Dorian 7
    C Egyptian 8
    C Enigmatic 8
    C Gypsy 8
    C Harmonic Minor 8
    C Hindu 8
    C Hirajoshi 8
    C Hungarian 8
    C Japanese 8
    C Locrian 9
    C Lydian 9
    C Major Blues 9
    C Major (Ionian) 9
    C Melodic Minor 9
    C Minor Blues 9
    C Mixolydian 9
    C Nine Tone 9
    C Oriental 10
    C Pentatonic Major 10
    C Pentatonic Minor 10
    C Persian 10
    C Phrygian 10
    C Romanian Minor 10
    C Spanish 8 Tone 10
    C Spanish Gypsy 10
    C Symmetric Dim. 1 11
    C Symmetric Dim. 2 11
Root note: C♯/D♭ 11
    C♯/D♭ Aeolian 11
    C♯/D♭ Algerian 11
    C♯/D♭ Arabic 11
    C♯/D♭ Bebop Dominant 11
    C♯/D♭ Bebop Major 12
    C♯/D♭ Bebop Minor 12
    C♯/D♭ Chinese 12
    C♯/D♭ Dorian 12
    C♯/D♭ Egyptian 12
    C♯/D♭ Enigmatic 12
    C♯/D♭ Gypsy 12
    C♯/D♭ Harmonic Minor 12
    C♯/D♭ Hindu 13
    C♯/D♭ Hirajoshi 13
    C♯/D♭ Hungarian 13
    C♯/D♭ Japanese 13

C♯/D♭ Locrian 13
C♯/D♭ Lydian 13
C♯/D♭ Major Blues 13
C♯/D♭ Major (Ionian) 13
C♯/D♭ Melodic Minor 14
C♯/D♭ Minor Blues 14
C♯/D♭ Mixolydian 14
C♯/D♭ Nine Tone 14
C♯/D♭ Oriental 14
C♯/D♭ Pentatonic Major 14
C♯/D♭ Pentatonic Minor 14
C♯/D♭ Persian 14
C♯/D♭ Phrygian 15
C♯/D♭ Romanian Minor 15
C♯/D♭ Spanish 8 Tone 15
C♯/D♭ Spanish Gypsy 15
C♯/D♭ Symmetric Dim. 1 15
C♯/D♭ Symmetric Dim. 2 15
Root note: D 15
D Aeolian 16
D Algerian 16
D Arabic 16
D Bebop Dominant 16
D Bebop Major 16
D Bebop Minor 16
D Chinese 16
D Dorian 16
D Egyptian 17
D Enigmatic 17
D Gypsy 17
D Harmonic Minor 17
D Hindu 17
D Hirajoshi 17
D Hungarian 17
D Japanese 17
D Locrian 18
D Lydian 18
D Major Blues 18
D Major (Ionian) 18
D Melodic Minor 18
D Minor Blues 18
D Mixolydian 18
D Nine Tone 18
D Oriental 19
D Pentatonic Major 19
D Pentatonic Minor 19
D Persian 19
D Phrygian 19
D Romanian Minor 19
D Spanish 8 Tone 19
D Spanish Gypsy 19
D Symmetric Dim. 1 20
D Symmetric Dim. 2 20
Root note: D♯/E♭ 20
D♯/E♭ Aeolian 20
D♯/E♭ Algerian 20
D♯/E♭ Arabic 20
D♯/E♭ Bebop Dominant 20
D♯/E♭ Bebop Major 21
D♯/E♭ Bebop Minor 21
D♯/E♭ Chinese 21
D♯/E♭ Dorian 21
D♯/E♭ Egyptian 21
D♯/E♭ Enigmatic 21
D♯/E♭ Gypsy 21
D♯/E♭ Harmonic Minor 21
D♯/E♭ Hindu 22
D♯/E♭ Hirajoshi 22
D♯/E♭ Hungarian 22
D♯/E♭ Japanese 22
D♯/E♭ Locrian 22
D♯/E♭ Lydian 22

4

D♯/E♭ Major Blues 22
D♯/E♭ Major (Ionian) 22
D♯/E♭ Melodic Minor 23
D♯/E♭ Minor Blues 23
D♯/E♭ Mixolydian 23
D♯/E♭ Nine Tone 23
D♯/E♭ Oriental 23
D♯/E♭ Pentatonic Major 23
D♯/E♭ Pentatonic Minor 23
D♯/E♭ Persian 23
D♯/E♭ Phrygian 24
D♯/E♭ Romanian Minor 24
D♯/E♭ Spanish 8 Tone 24
D♯/E♭ Spanish Gypsy 24
D♯/E♭ Symmetric Dim. 1 24
D♯/E♭ Symmetric Dim. 2 24
Root note: E 24
E Aeolian 25
E Algerian 25
E Arabic 25
E Bebop Dominant 25
E Bebop Major 25
E Bebop Minor 25
E Chinese 25
E Dorian 25
E Egyptian 26
E Enigmatic 26
E Gypsy 26
E Harmonic Minor 26
E Hindu 26
E Hirajoshi 26
E Hungarian 26
E Japanese 26
E Locrian 27
E Lydian 27
E Major Blues 27
E Major (Ionian) 27
E Melodic Minor 27
E Minor Blues 27
E Mixolydian 27
E Nine Tone 27
E Oriental 28
E Pentatonic Major 28
E Pentatonic Minor 28
E Persian 28
E Phrygian 28
E Romanian Minor 28
E Spanish 8 Tone 28
E Spanish Gypsy 28
E Symmetric Dim. 1 29
E Symmetric Dim. 2 29
Root note: F 29
F Aeolian 29
F Algerian 29
F Arabic 29
F Bebop Dominant 29
F Bebop Major 30
F Bebop Minor 30
F Chinese 30
F Dorian 30
F Egyptian 30
F Enigmatic 30
F Gypsy 30
F Harmonic Minor 30
F Hindu 31
F Hirajoshi 31
F Hungarian 31
F Japanese 31
F Locrian 31
F Lydian 31
F Major Blues 31
F Major (Ionian) 31

F Melodic Minor 32
F Minor Blues 32
F Mixolydian 32
F Nine Tone 32
F Oriental 32
F Pentatonic Major 32
F Pentatonic Minor 32
F Persian 32
F Phrygian 33
F Romanian Minor 33
F Spanish 8 Tone 33
F Spanish Gypsy 33
F Symmetric Dim. 1 33
F Symmetric Dim. 2 33
Root note: F♯/G♭ 33
F♯/G♭ Aeolian 34
F♯/G♭ Algerian 34
F♯/G♭ Arabic 34
F♯/G♭ Bebop Dominant 34
F♯/G♭ Bebop Major 34
F♯/G♭ Bebop Minor 34
F♯/G♭ Chinese 34
F♯/G♭ Dorian 34
F♯/G♭ Egyptian 35
F♯/G♭ Enigmatic 35
F♯/G♭ Gypsy 35
F♯/G♭ Harmonic Minor 35
F♯/G♭ Hindu 35
F♯/G♭ Hirajoshi 35
F♯/G♭ Hungarian 35
F♯/G♭ Japanese 35
F♯/G♭ Locrian 36
F♯/G♭ Lydian 36
F♯/G♭ Major Blues 36
F♯/G♭ Major (Ionian) 36
F♯/G♭ Melodic Minor 36
F♯/G♭ Minor Blues 36
F♯/G♭ Mixolydian 36
F♯/G♭ Nine Tone 36
F♯/G♭ Oriental 37
F♯/G♭ Pentatonic Major 37
F♯/G♭ Pentatonic Minor 37
F♯/G♭ Persian 37
F♯/G♭ Phrygian 37
F♯/G♭ Romanian Minor 37
F♯/G♭ Spanish 8 Tone 37
F♯/G♭ Spanish Gypsy 37
F♯/G♭ Symmetric Dim. 1 38
F♯/G♭ Symmetric Dim. 2 38
Root note: G 38
G Aeolian 38
G Algerian 38
G Arabic 38
G Bebop Dominant 38
G Bebop Major 39
G Bebop Minor 39
G Chinese 39
G Dorian 39
G Egyptian 39
G Enigmatic 39
G Gypsy 39
G Harmonic Minor 39
G Hindu 40
G Hirajoshi 40
G Hungarian 40
G Japanese 40
G Locrian 40
G Lydian 40
G Major Blues 40
G Major (Ionian) 40
G Melodic Minor 41
G Minor Blues 41

G Mixolydian 41
G Nine Tone 41
G Oriental 41
G Pentatonic Major 41
G Pentatonic Minor 41
G Persian 41
G Phrygian 42
G Romanian Minor 42
G Spanish 8 Tone 42
G Spanish Gypsy 42
G Symmetric Dim. 1 42
G Symmetric Dim. 2 42
Root note: G♯/A♭ 42
G♯/A♭ Aeolian 43
G♯/A♭ Algerian 43
G♯/A♭ Arabic 43
G♯/A♭ Bebop Dominant 43
G♯/A♭ Bebop Major 43
G♯/A♭ Bebop Minor 43
G♯/A♭ Chinese 43
G♯/A♭ Dorian 43
G♯/A♭ Egyptian 44
G♯/A♭ Enigmatic 44
G♯/A♭ Gypsy 44
G♯/A♭ Harmonic Minor 44
G♯/A♭ Hindu 44
G♯/A♭ Hirajoshi 44
G♯/A♭ Hungarian 44
G♯/A♭ Japanese 44
G♯/A♭ Locrian 45
G♯/A♭ Lydian 45
G♯/A♭ Major Blues 45
G♯/A♭ Major (Ionian) 45
G♯/A♭ Melodic Minor 45
G♯/A♭ Minor Blues 45
G♯/A♭ Mixolydian 45
G♯/A♭ Nine Tone 45
G♯/A♭ Oriental 46
G♯/A♭ Pentatonic Major 46
G♯/A♭ Pentatonic Minor 46
G♯/A♭ Persian 46
G♯/A♭ Phrygian 46
G♯/A♭ Romanian Minor 46
G♯/A♭ Spanish 8 Tone 46
G♯/A♭ Spanish Gypsy 46
G♯/A♭ Symmetric Dim. 1 47
G♯/A♭ Symmetric Dim. 2 47
Root note: A 47
A Aeolian 47
A Algerian 47
A Arabic 47
A Bebop Dominant 47
A Bebop Major 48
A Bebop Minor 48
A Chinese 48
A Dorian 48
A Egyptian 48
A Enigmatic 48
A Gypsy 48
A Harmonic Minor 48
A Hindu 49
A Hirajoshi 49
A Hungarian 49
A Japanese 49
A Locrian 49
A Lydian 49
A Major Blues 49
A Major (Ionian) 49
A Melodic Minor 50
A Minor Blues 50
A Mixolydian 50
A Nine Tone 50

A Oriental 50
A Pentatonic Major 50
A Pentatonic Minor 50
A Persian 50
A Phrygian 51
A Romanian Minor 51
A Spanish 8 Tone 51
A Spanish Gypsy 51
A Symmetric Dim. 1 51
A Symmetric Dim. 2 51
Root note: A♯/B♭ 51
A♯/B♭ Aeolian 52
A♯/B♭ Algerian 52
A♯/B♭ Arabic 52
A♯/B♭ Bebop Dominant 52
A♯/B♭ Bebop Major 52
A♯/B♭ Bebop Minor 52
A♯/B♭ Chinese 52
A♯/B♭ Dorian 52
A♯/B♭ Egyptian 53
A♯/B♭ Enigmatic 53
A♯/B♭ Gypsy 53
A♯/B♭ Harmonic Minor 53
A♯/B♭ Hindu 53
A♯/B♭ Hirajoshi 53
A♯/B♭ Hungarian 53
A♯/B♭ Japanese 53
A♯/B♭ Locrian 54
A♯/B♭ Lydian 54
A♯/B♭ Major Blues 54
A♯/B♭ Major (Ionian) 54
A♯/B♭ Melodic Minor 54
A♯/B♭ Minor Blues 54
A♯/B♭ Mixolydian 54
A♯/B♭ Nine Tone 54
A♯/B♭ Oriental 55
A♯/B♭ Pentatonic Major 55
A♯/B♭ Pentatonic Minor 55
A♯/B♭ Persian 55
A♯/B♭ Phrygian 55
A♯/B♭ Romanian Minor 55
A♯/B♭ Spanish 8 Tone 55
A♯/B♭ Spanish Gypsy 55
A♯/B♭ Symmetric Dim. 1 56
A♯/B♭ Symmetric Dim. 2 56
Root note: B 56
B Aeolian 56
B Algerian 56
B Arabic 56
B Bebop Dominant 56
B Bebop Major 57
B Bebop Minor 57
B Chinese 57
B Dorian 57
B Egyptian 57
B Enigmatic 57
B Gypsy 57
B Harmonic Minor 57
B Hindu 58
B Hirajoshi 58
B Hungarian 58
B Japanese 58
B Locrian 58
B Lydian 58
B Major Blues 58
B Major (Ionian) 58
B Melodic Minor 59
B Minor Blues 59
B Mixolydian 59
B Nine Tone 59
B Oriental 59
B Pentatonic Major 59

      B Pentatonic Minor 59
      B Persian 59
      B Phrygian 60
      B Romanian Minor 60
      B Spanish 8 Tone 60
      B Spanish Gypsy 60
      B Symmetric Dim. 1 60
      B Symmetric Dim. 2 60
Movable 'Box' Scale Patterns 61
      Aeolian 61
      Algerian 61
      Arabic 61
      Bebop Dominant 62
      Bebop Major 62
      Bebop Minor 62
      Chinese 62
      Dorian 63
      Egyptian 63
      Enigmatic 63
      Gypsy 63
      Harmonic Minor 64
      Hindu 64
      Hirajoshi 64
      Hungarian 64
      Japanese 65
      Locrian 65
      Lydian 65
      Major Blues 65
      Major (Ionian) 66
      Melodic Minor 66
      Minor Blues 66
      Mixolydian 66
      Nine Tone 67
      Oriental 67
      Pentatonic Major 67
      Pentatonic Minor 67
      Persian 68
      Phrygian 68
      Romanian Minor 68
      Spanish 8 Tone 68
      Spanish Gypsy 69
      Symmetric Dim. 1 69
      Symmetric Dim. 2 69

The Aims of This Book

"I promise if you work on scales for two hours a day for two years, you will become a fine [cellist / insert instrument of your choice?]. I keep my promises." Hans 'Enke' Zentgraf.

The aim of this book is not to present you with a method for learning your scales faster. Like Hans Zentgraf, I do not believe the road to becoming a better musician can be navigated at great speed. For the average person with other things to be done during the day, two hours per day on scales practise alone[1] represents **a lot of work** and moreover, **commitment**, right? The way to learn your scales faster is by practising them more often, in greater variety and over the full range of positions on the fingerboard.

This book will provide you with the raw ingredients to help you to learn a wide variety of scales and modes, it is up to you to put in the work to learn these scales and to learn how to use them effectively in context. Everybody learns differently and (thankfully) plays differently; with this book, the information you need to master a scale is at your fingertips.

I wish you the best of luck and, most importantly, enjoyment in the **process** of learning.

Why Learn to Play Scales?

Learning to play a variety of scales makes you a better musician. **It teaches your fingers** where to find and how to handle the different positions you might encounter when playing pieces of music, **it trains your musical ear** by helping you to learn to recognise intervals and how they relate to finger positioning, and ultimately **it trains your musical brain** how to recognise different musical colours and eventually create them on the fly.

How to Use This Book

A picture is worth a thousand words.

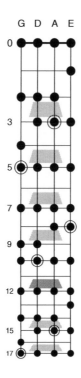

Figure 1: Example figure showing the position of the notes of the C major scale.

The primary purpose of this book is to help you visualise the locations of the notes of a scale on the banjo fingerboard, a typical diagram in the book is shown in Figure 1. This particular page gives you information about the C Major scale. It shows the position of the notes of the C Major scale up to the position on the fingerboard 17 semitones above the nut.

---

[1]Note that scales practise should form only part of your practise regime.

10

On the **left hand side of the diagram**, you will see numbers from 0 (the nut) to 17: these represent the number of semitones above the nut each horizontal line corresponds to. On a fretted instrument, the **horizontal lines** would correspond to frets, but if you have bought this book for use with an instrument without frets or fret markings, then you need to use your mind's eye to visualise these positions (doing so is an excellent mental exercise). The diagrams are scaled so that the location of the horizontal lines is in proportion to where they would appear on a real instrument, this will help you see visually and thus anticipate physically the contraction in finger spacing required in moving the scale further up the neck of the instrument. The large **solid dots** in the main diagram show the locations of the notes of the scale in question. **Ringed dots** show the location of the root notes of the scale. Also provided with each fingerboard diagram are the notes in score notation and the defining intervals of each scale, which follow the key given in Table 1. For example, the Ionian mode (or major scale) would be notated: T T S T T T S.

Using Scale Diagrams to Construct Exercises

Exactly in which order you need to play the notes of a given scale over a given number of octaves I leave to you, the reader. This is part of the purpose of this book – to give you ideas about the various ways you could finger a scale, or musical phrase. The movable box scales can be used to see how a scale might be played in a particular position on the neck. The full fingerboard diagrams can be used to see how these box patterns can be connected together, or to help you develop your own scale fingerings, which might include shifts.

Notation	Interval
S	Semitone / Augmented unison
T	Tone / Major 2nd
m3	Minor 3rd
M3	Major 3rd
p4	Perfect 4th
d5	Diminished 5th
p5	Perfect 5th
m6	Minor 6th
M6	Major 6th
m7	Minor 7th
M7	Major 7th

Table 1: Key to interval notation.

Typical exercises you could develop include:

- playing the scale over a given number of octaves in ascending and then descending order;

- playing the scale in sequences e.g. if '1' and '2' denote the first and second notes of the scale etc. then the sequences 1,2,3, 2,3,4, 3,4,5, 4,5,6, 5,6,7, 6,7,8, 8,7,6, 7,6,5, 6,5,4, 5,4,3, 4,3,2, 3,2,1 or 1,2,3,1, 2,3,4,2, 3,4,5,3, 4,5,6,4 etc. might provide a good starting point;

- playing the scale and skipping over some notes e.g. using the notation above: 1,3,5,7,8,6,4,2;

- using a background drone note set to the pitch of the root note of the scale, experiment by improvising phrases, or executing scale sequences to see how they sound in context.

The possibilities are endless! My advice would be to construct sequences based around the scale patterns you are trying to learn that appear in real pieces of music. You should also add variation to your practising of scales by changing the timing of notes (e.g. playing them at an even tempo, in triplets, sixteenths, or with a galloping or syncopated rhythm), and phrasing (e.g. emphasising distinct notes, or slurring, or a combination). Recall that for the melodic minor scale (a.k.a. 'Jazz Minor'), the notes ascending and descending are different.

Author's Notes on this Edition

To avoid over-cluttering the diagrams, I have not included the names of the notes (or scale degrees) on the fingerboard diagrams. I have, however, included for each scale the notes in score notation. In all cases, I have elected to use sharps to indicate accidentals. The reason for this is that these scales could appear in any key and technically, the precise choice of accidentals as a combination of sharps and/or flats would be determined by the key of the piece at the point the notes appeared in the music. To present all possible enharmonic equivalents would not be an efficient use of space.

I welcome **constructive** feedback on my book. Please feel free to contact me with comments by email using the address benjamin.cello.mad.taylor@googlemail.com. In particular, if you would like a scales or arpeggios book, for a stringed instrument in an unusual tuning, please don't hesitate to let me know.

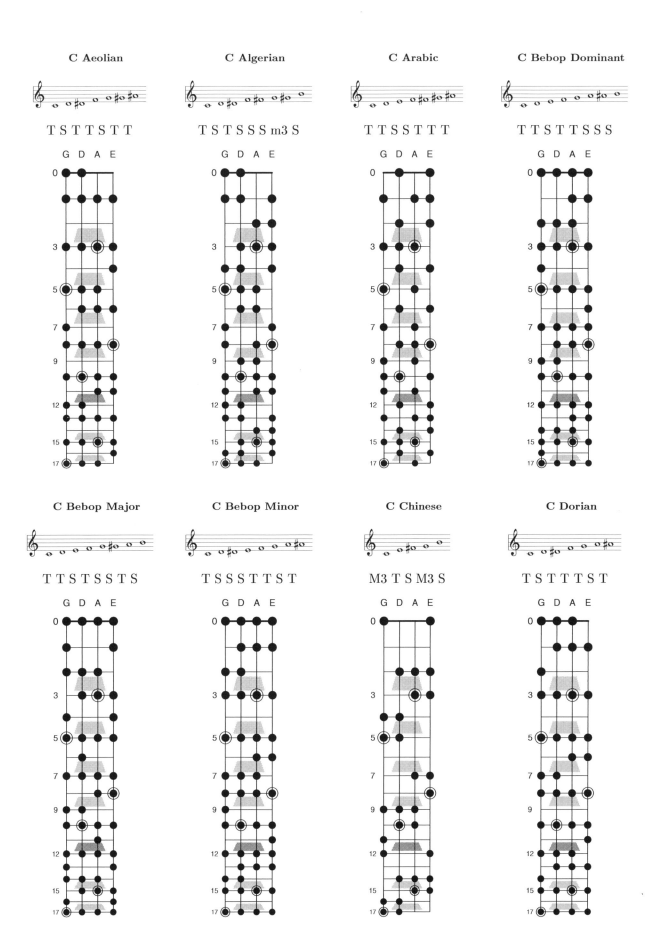

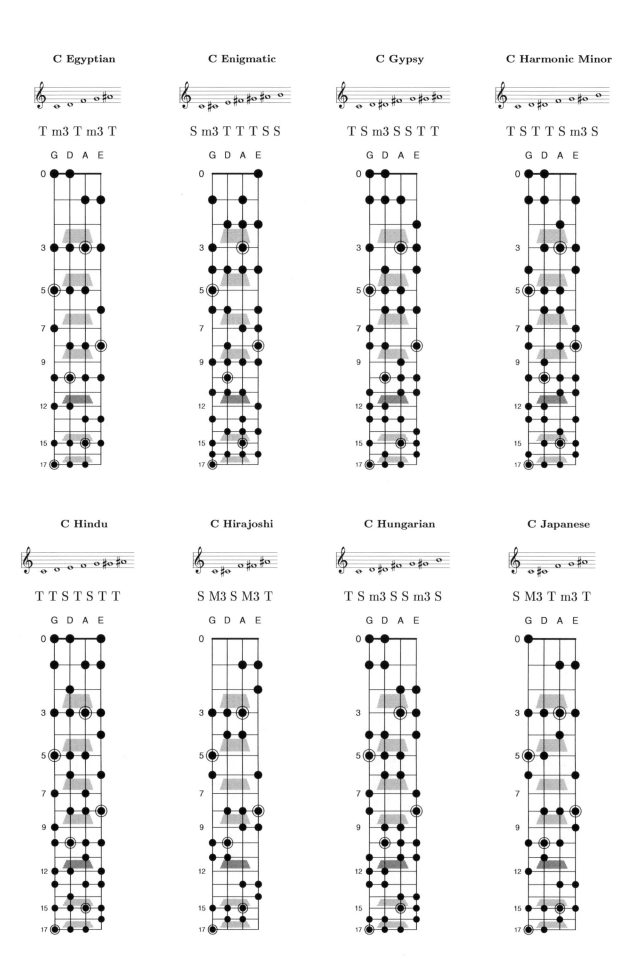

14

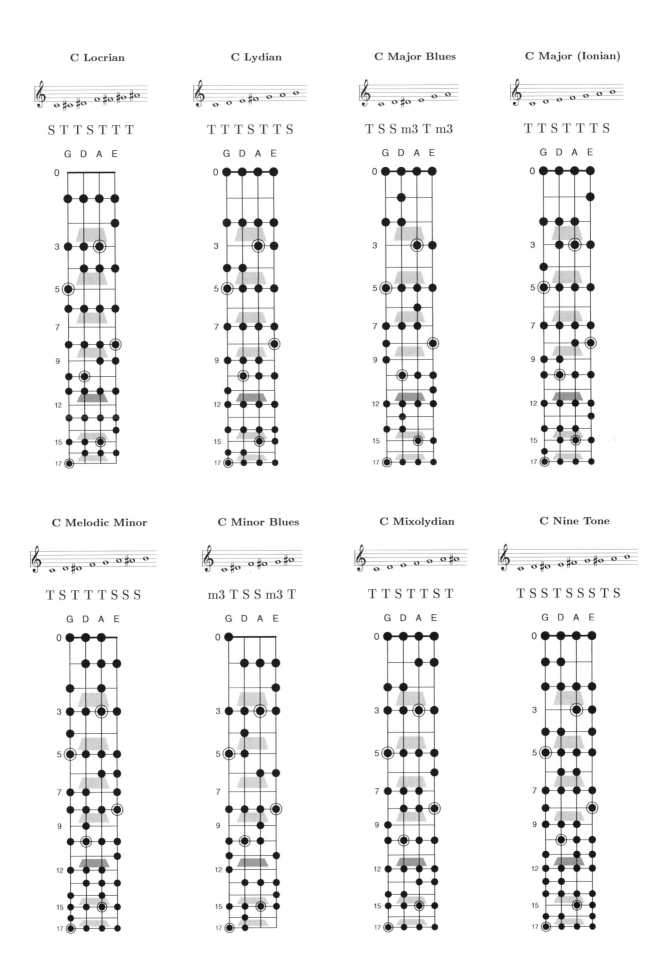

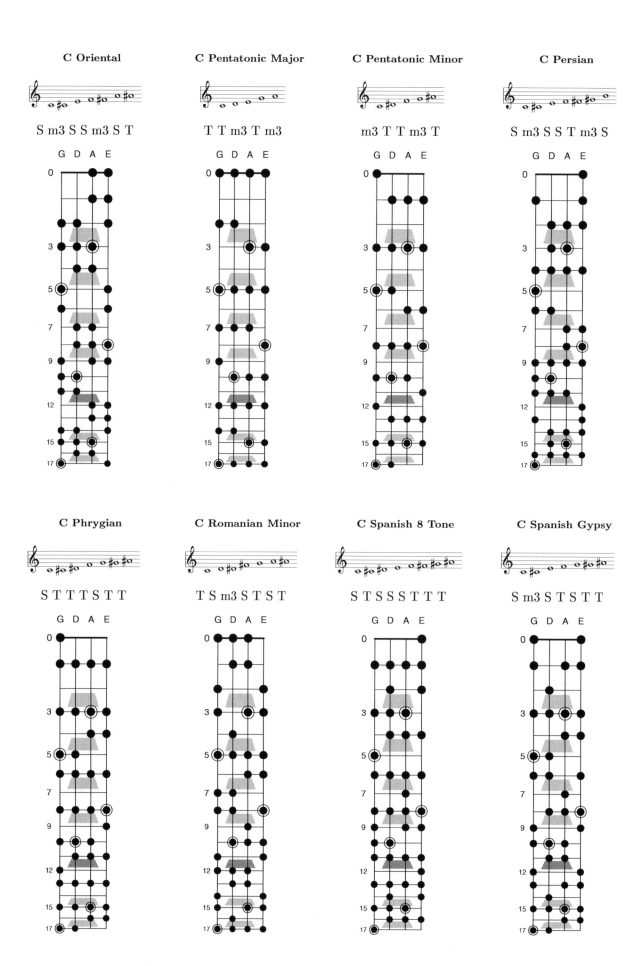

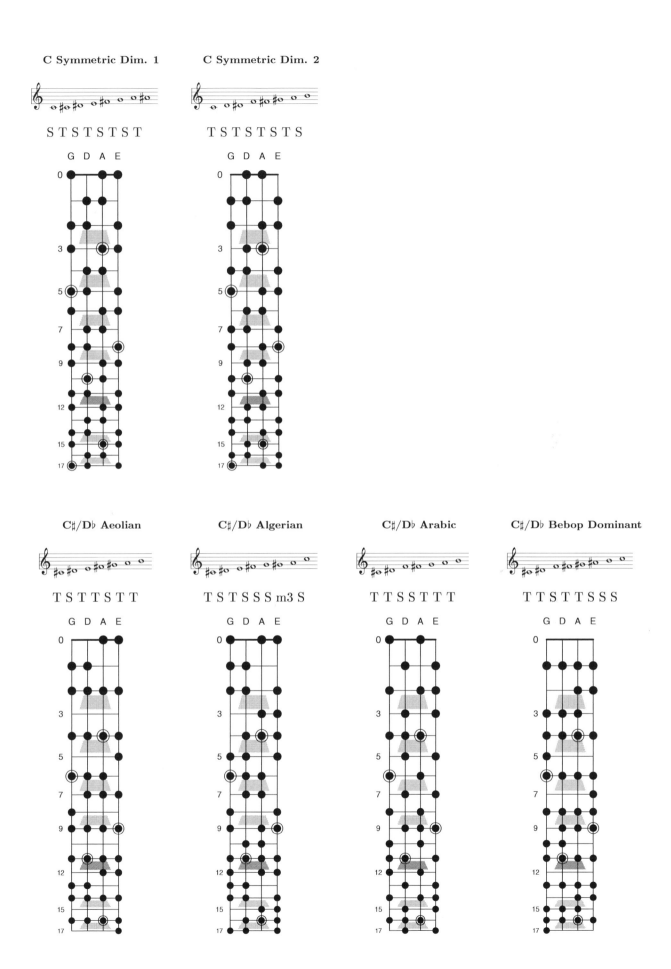

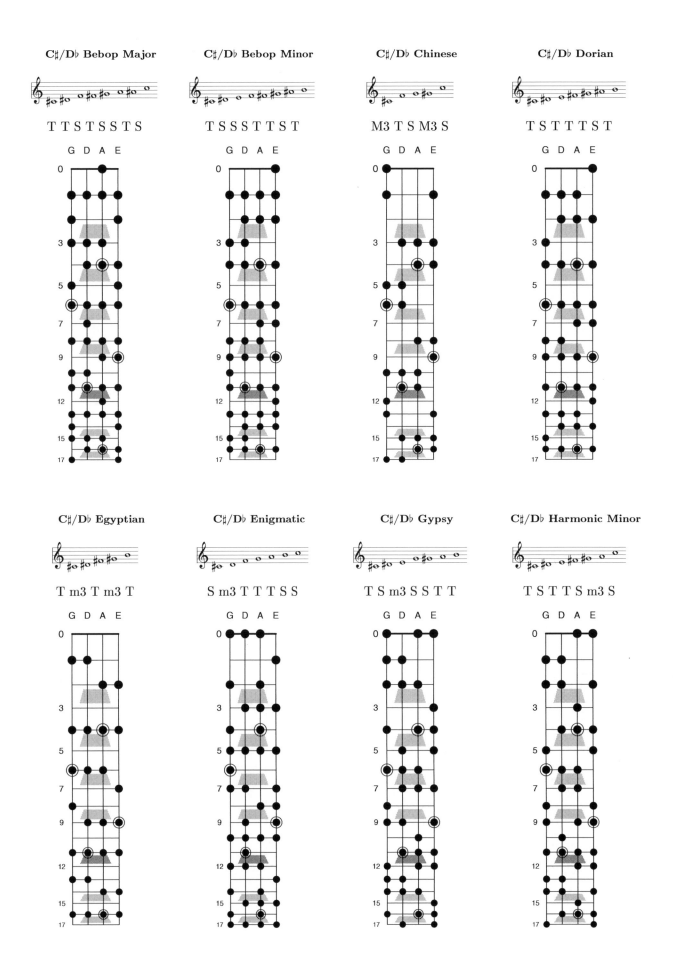

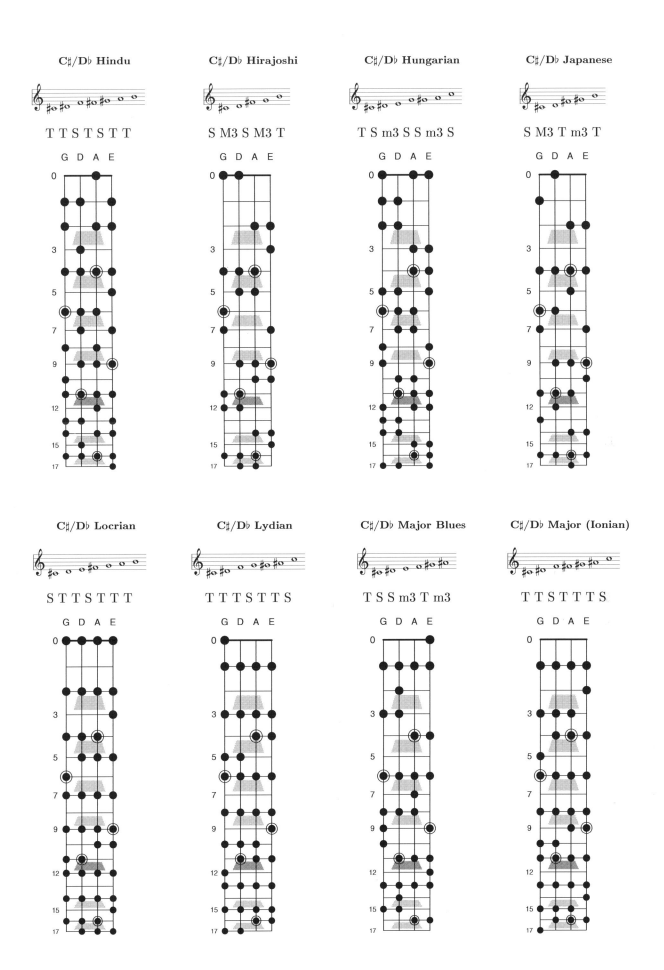

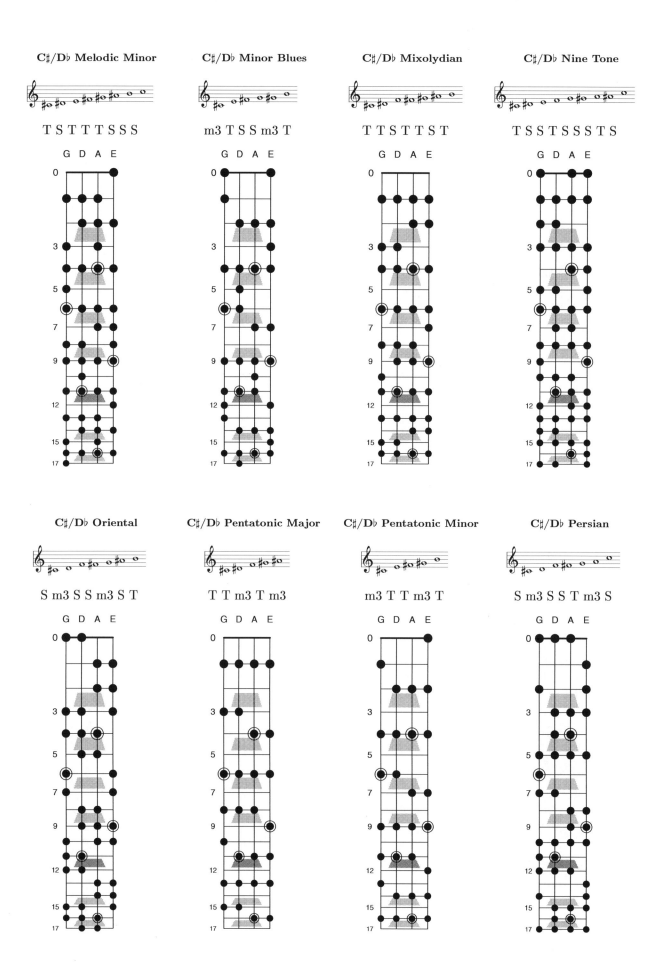

C♯/D♭ Phrygian

S T T T S T T

C♯/D♭ Romanian Minor

T S m3 S T S T

C♯/D♭ Spanish 8 Tone

S T S S S T T

C♯/D♭ Spanish Gypsy

S m3 S T S T T

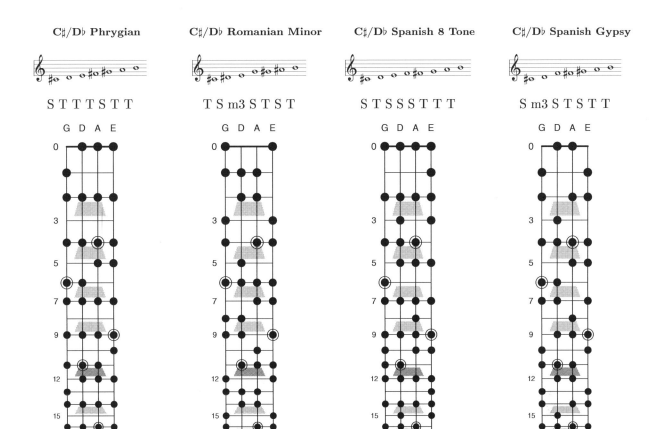

C♯/D♭ Symmetric Dim. 1

S T S T S T S T

C♯/D♭ Symmetric Dim. 2

T S T S T S T S

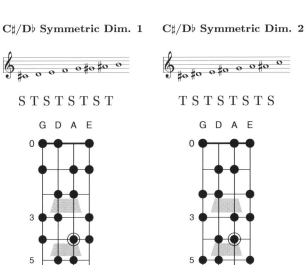

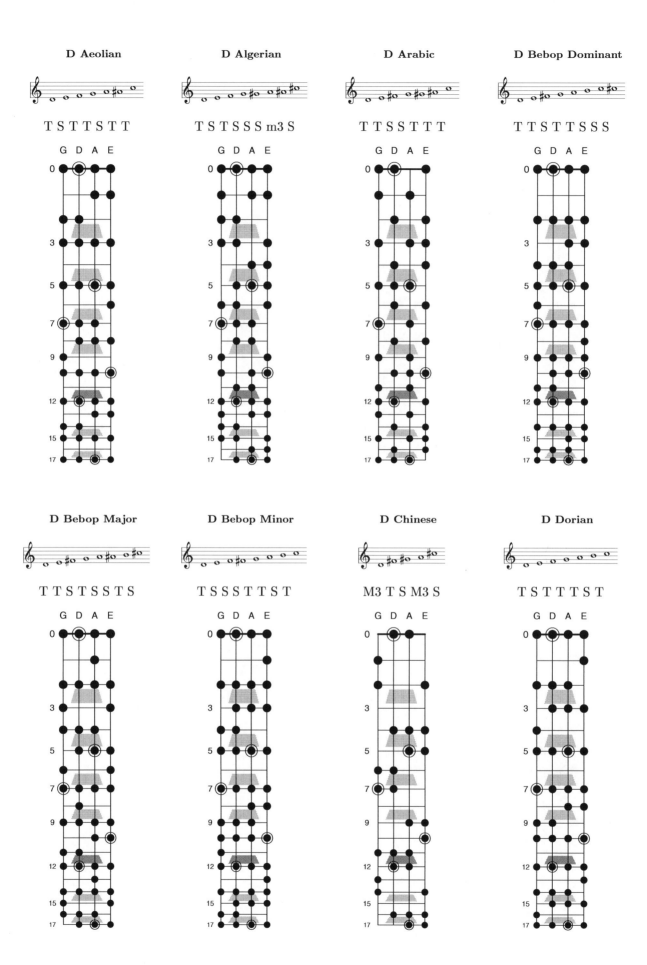

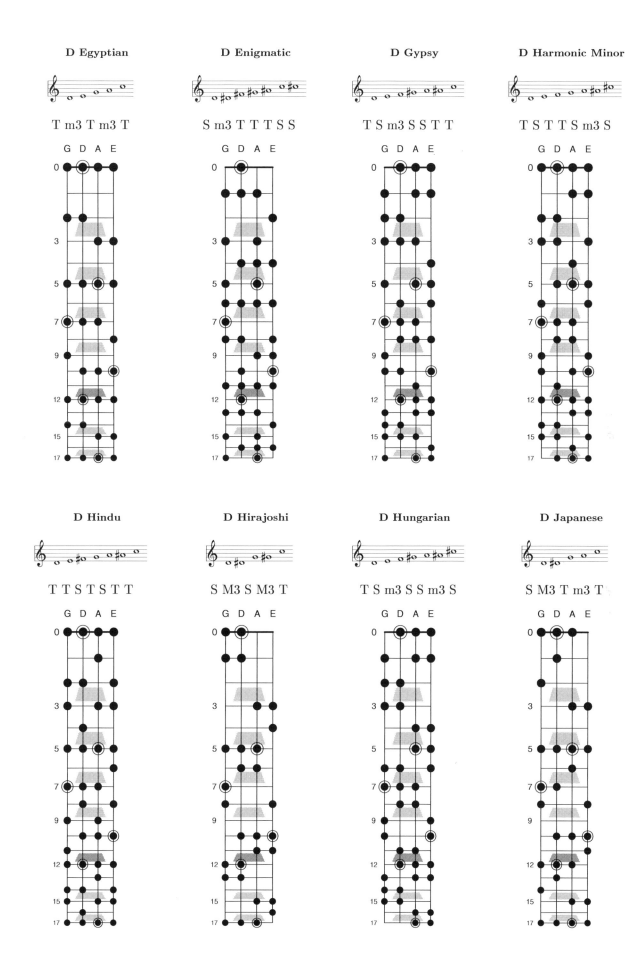

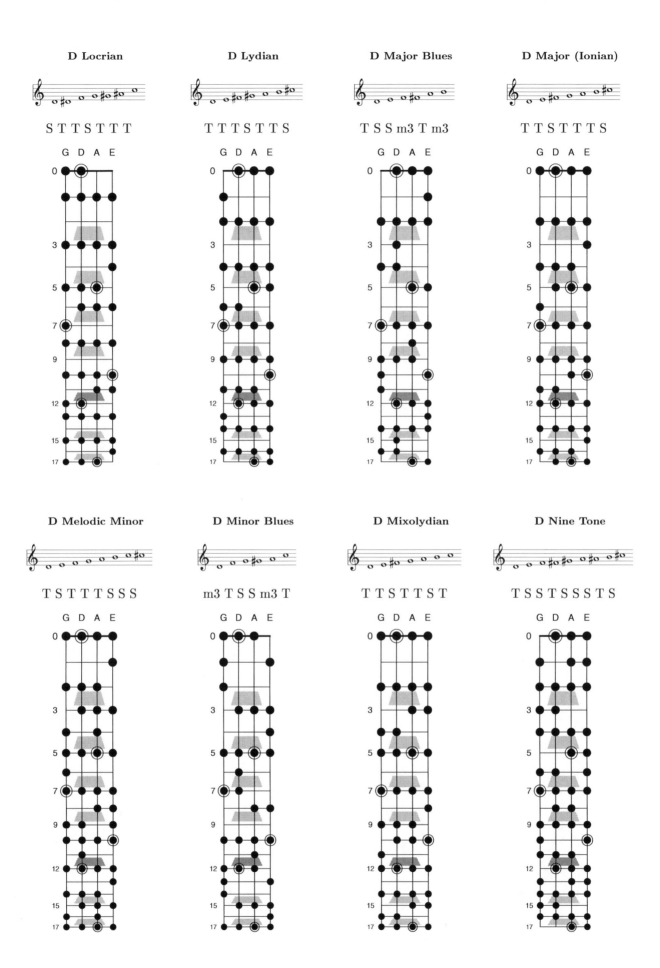

24

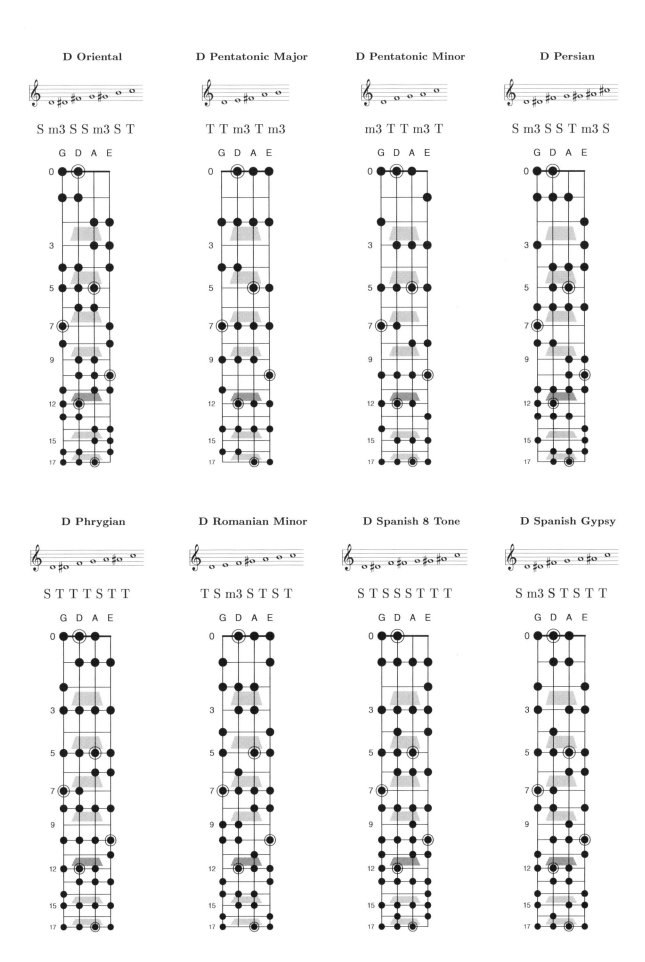

D Symmetric Dim. 1

S T S T S T S T

D Symmetric Dim. 2

T S T S T S T S

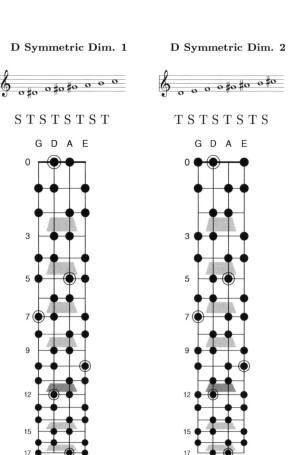

D♯/E♭ Aeolian

T S T T S T T

D♯/E♭ Algerian

T S T S S S m3 S

D♯/E♭ Arabic

T T S S T T T

D♯/E♭ Bebop Dominant

T T S T T S S S

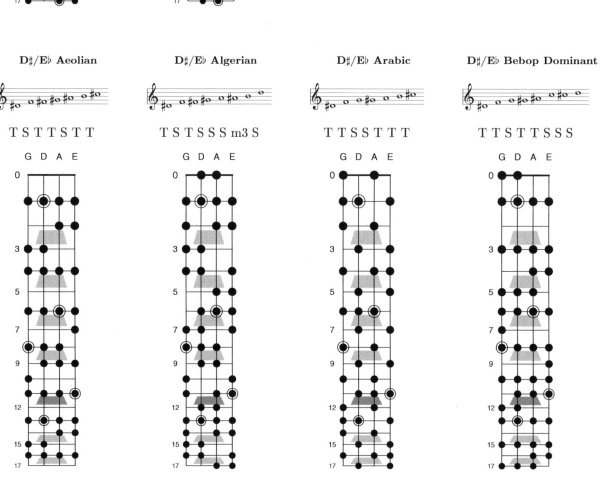

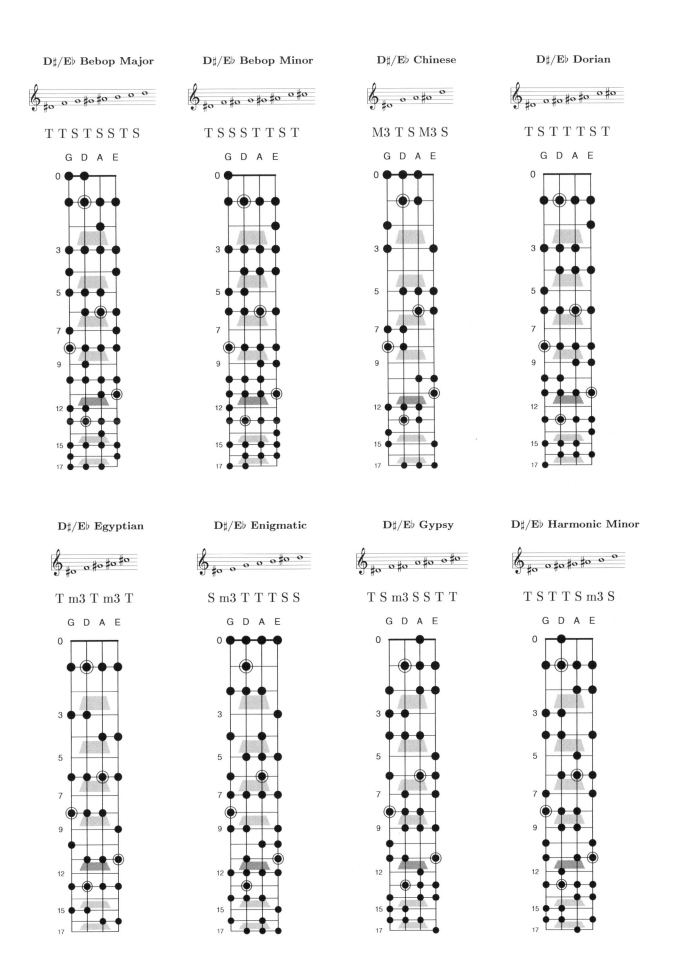

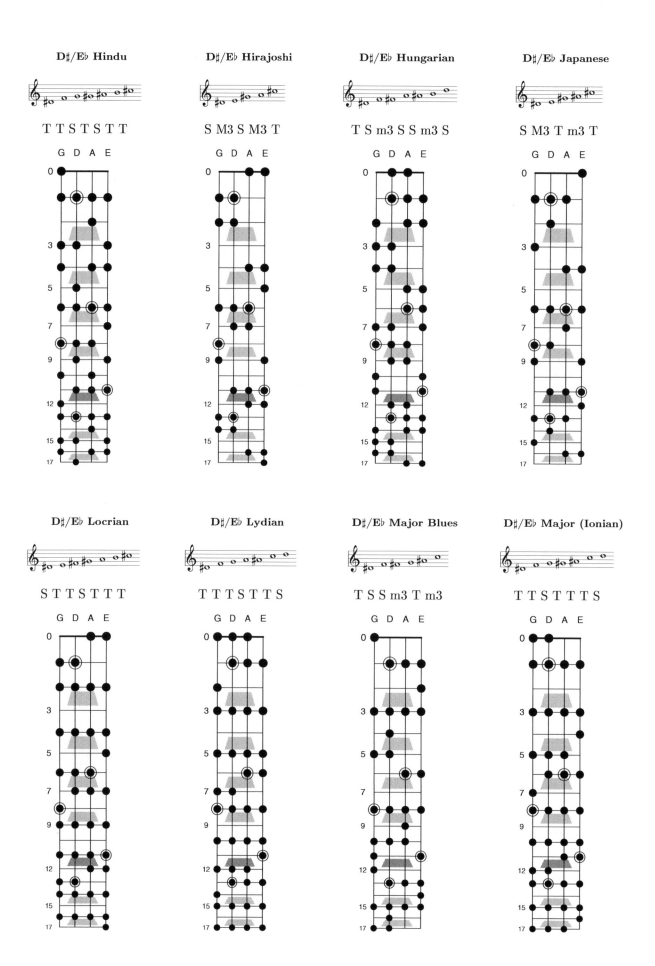

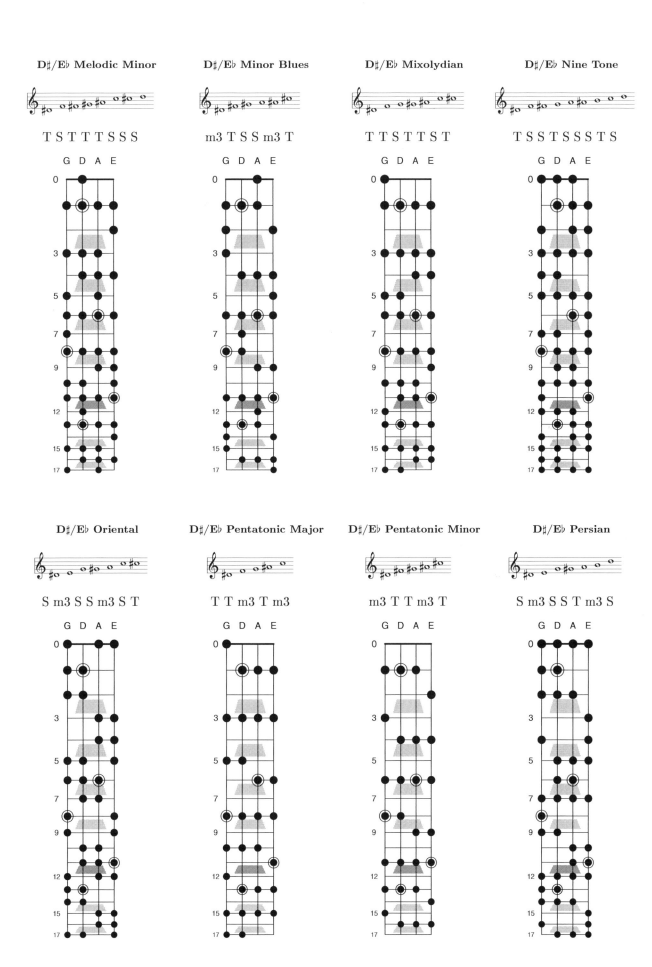

D♯/E♭ Phrygian

S T T T S T T

D♯/E♭ Romanian Minor

T S m3 S T S T

D♯/E♭ Spanish 8 Tone

S T S S S T T T

D♯/E♭ Spanish Gypsy

S m3 S T S T T

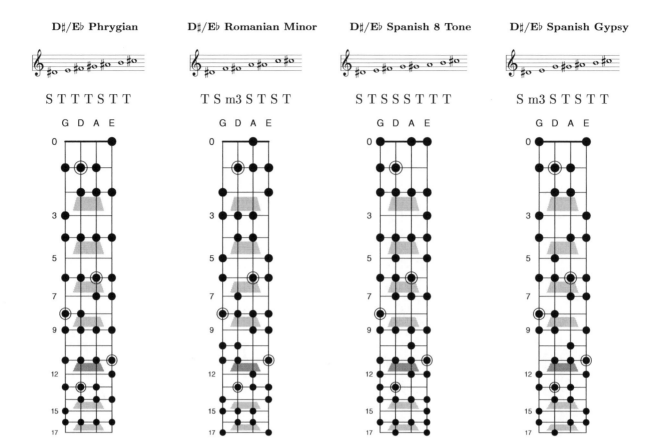

D♯/E♭ Symmetric Dim. 1

S T S T S T S T

D♯/E♭ Symmetric Dim. 2

T S T S T S T S

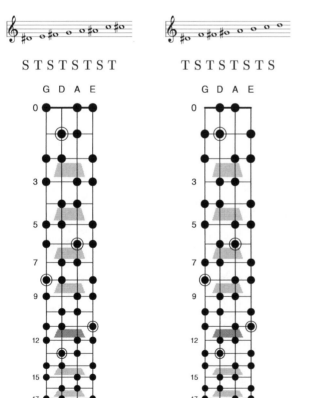

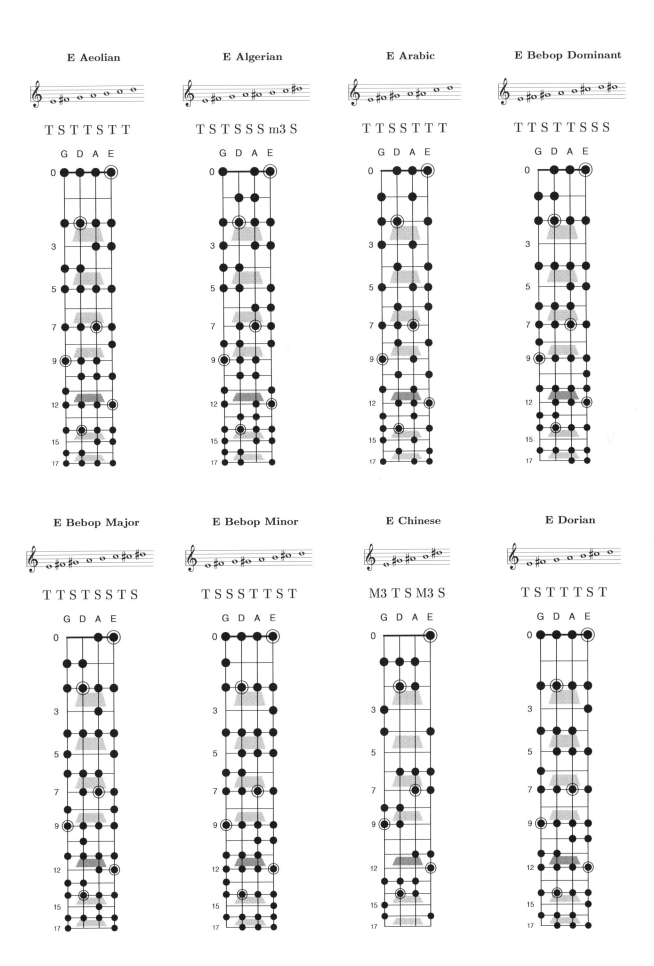

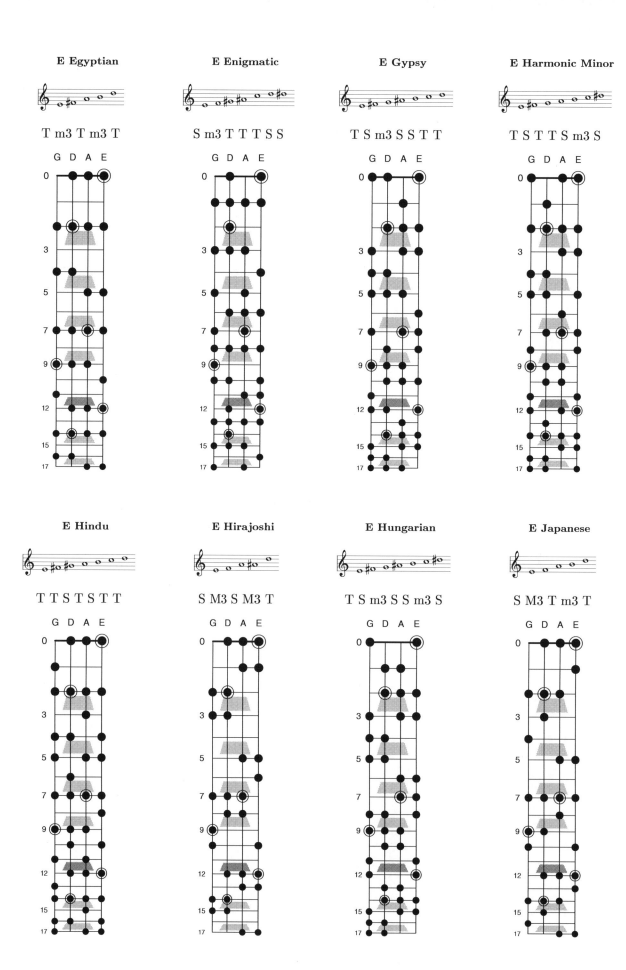

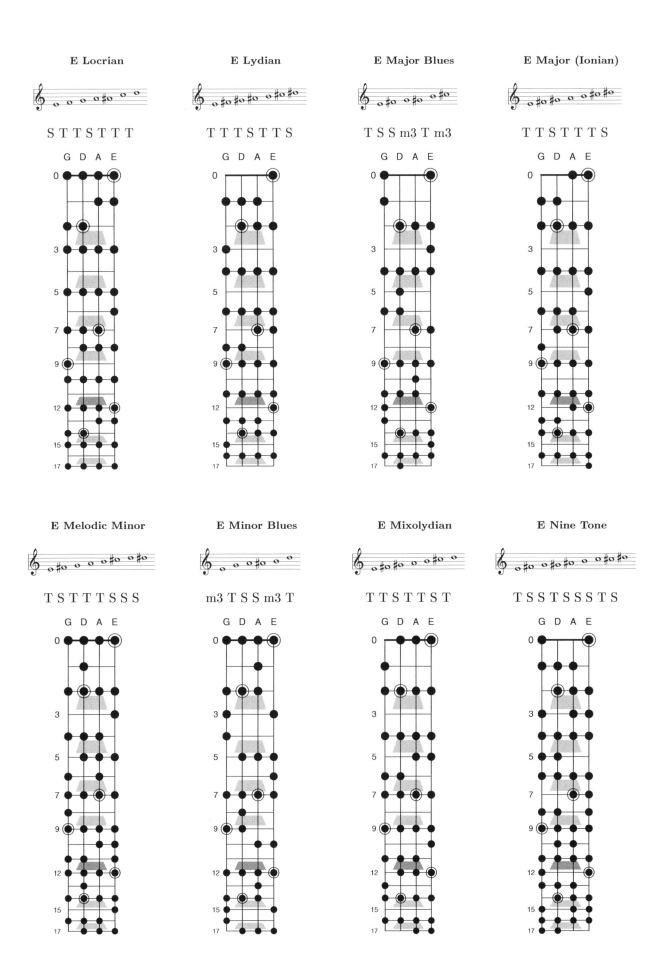

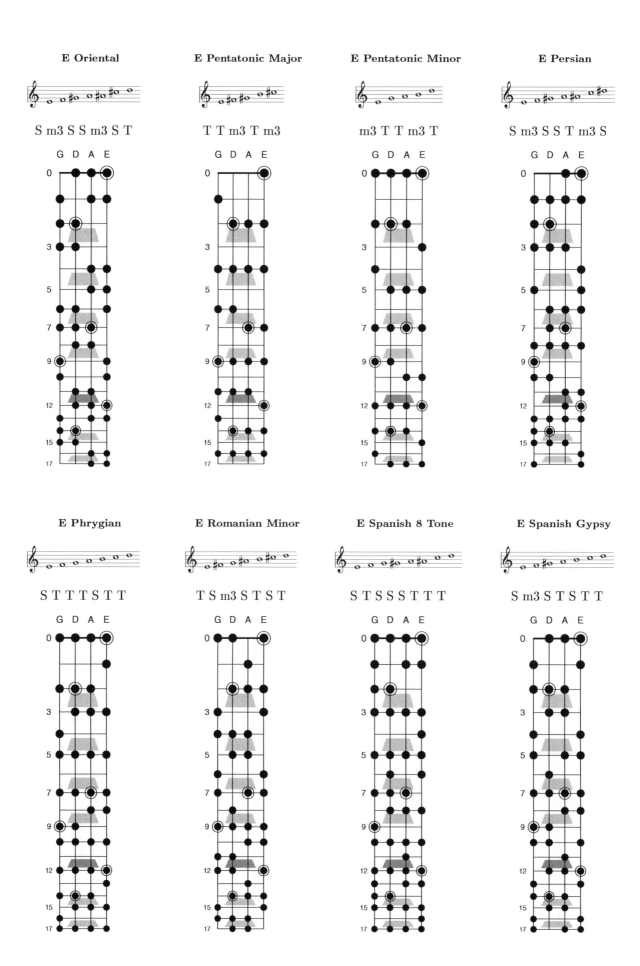

34

E Symmetric Dim. 1

S T S T S T S T

E Symmetric Dim. 2

T S T S T S T S

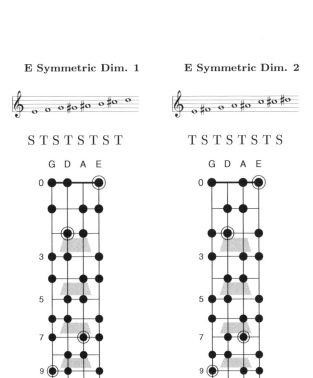

F Aeolian

T S T T S T T

F Algerian

T S T S S S m3 S

F Arabic

T T S S T T T

F Bebop Dominant

T T S T T S S S

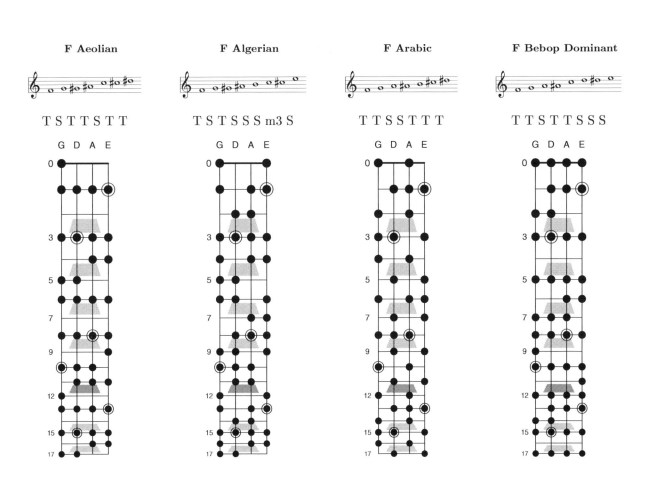

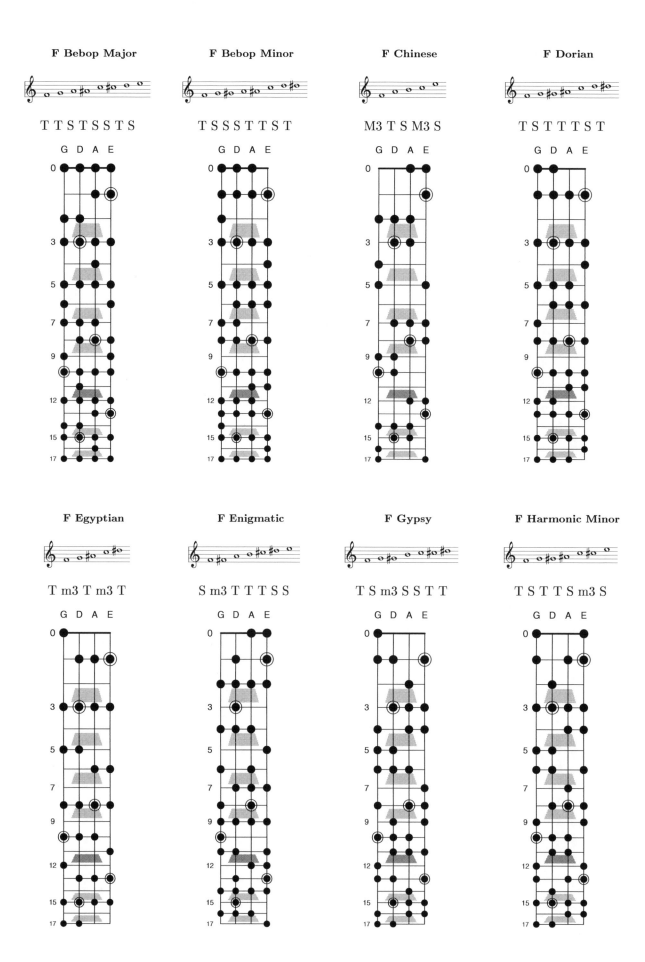

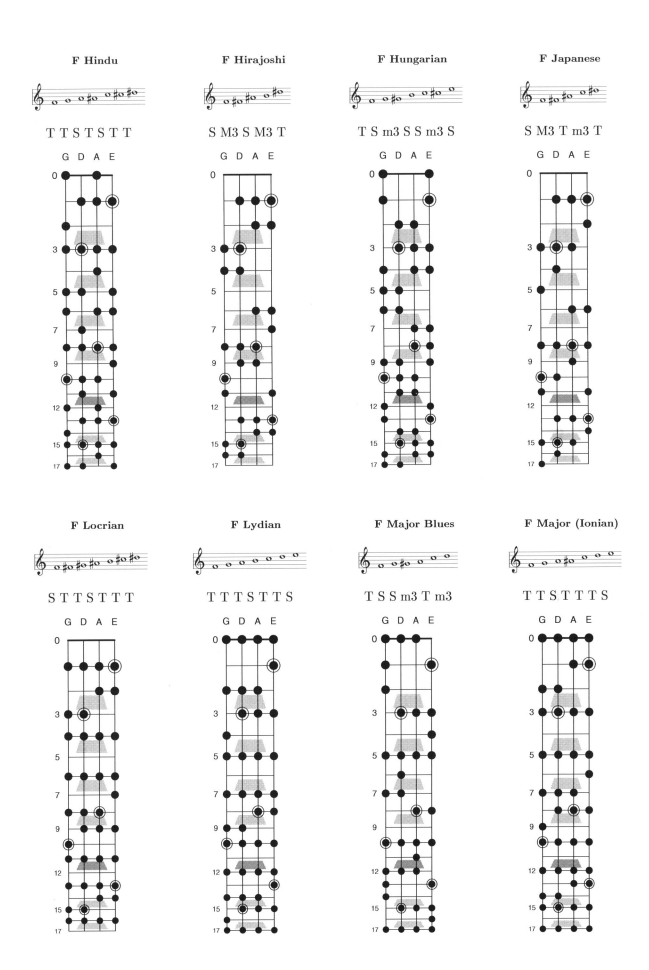

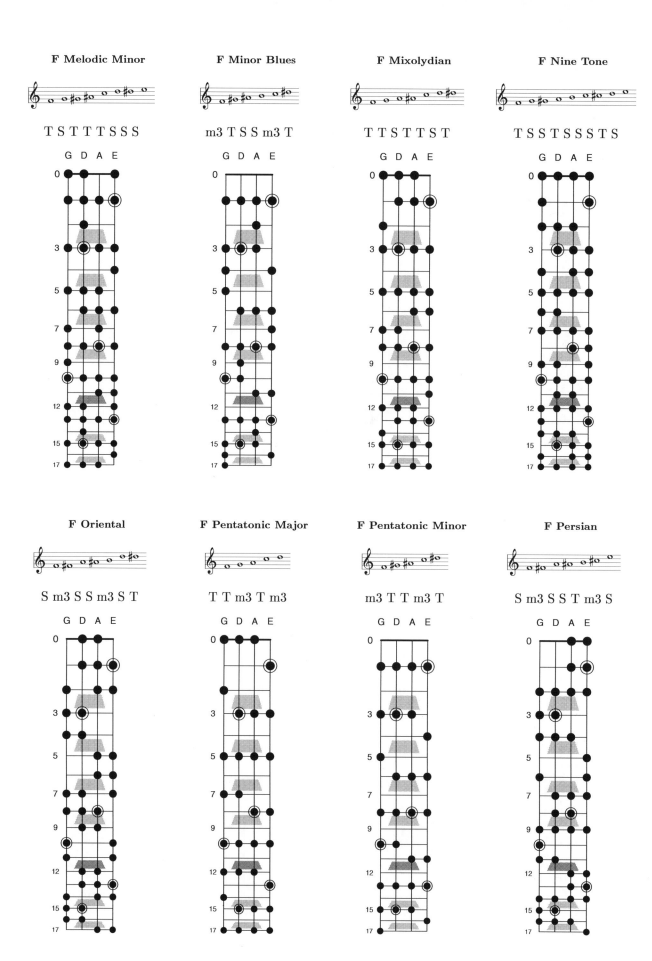

F Phrygian **F Romanian Minor** **F Spanish 8 Tone** **F Spanish Gypsy**

S T T T S T T   T S m3 S T S T   S T S S S T T T   S m3 S T S T T

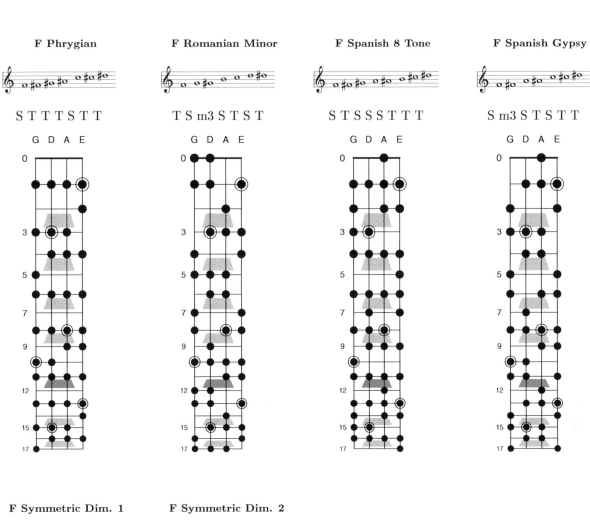

F Symmetric Dim. 1 **F Symmetric Dim. 2**

S T S T S T S T   T S T S T S T S

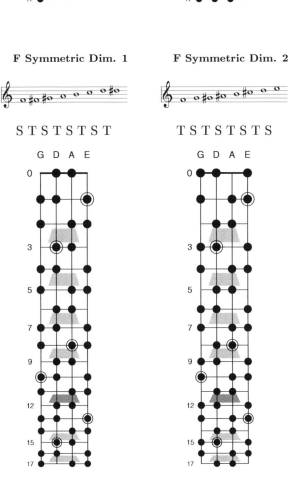

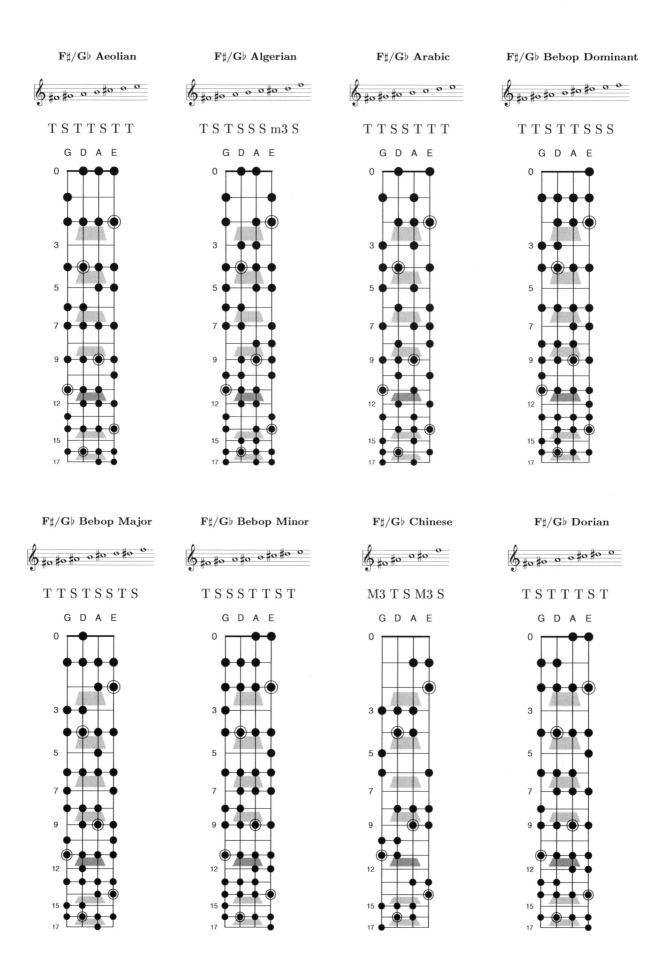

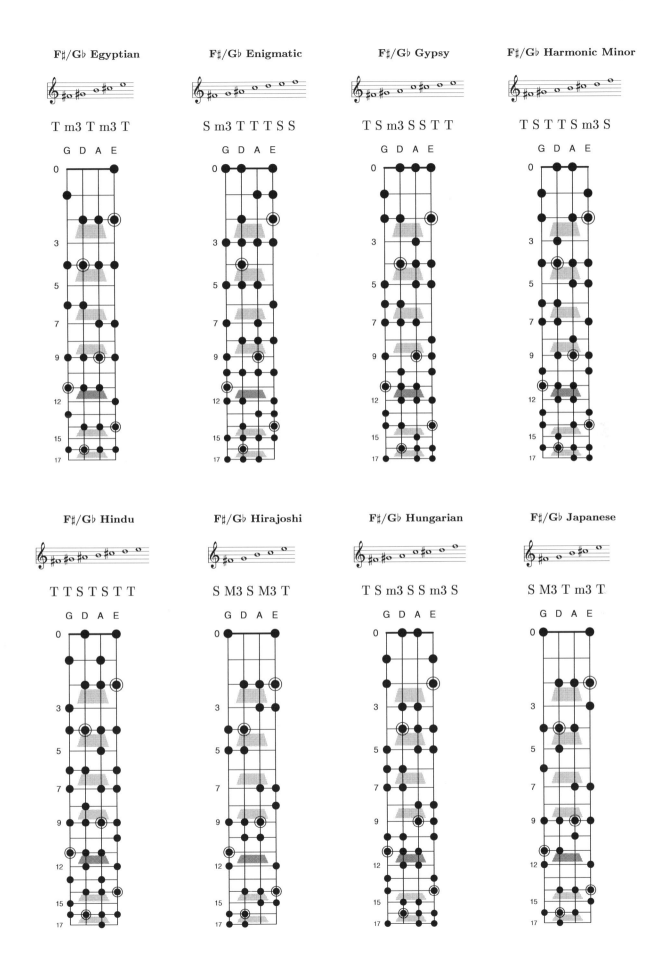

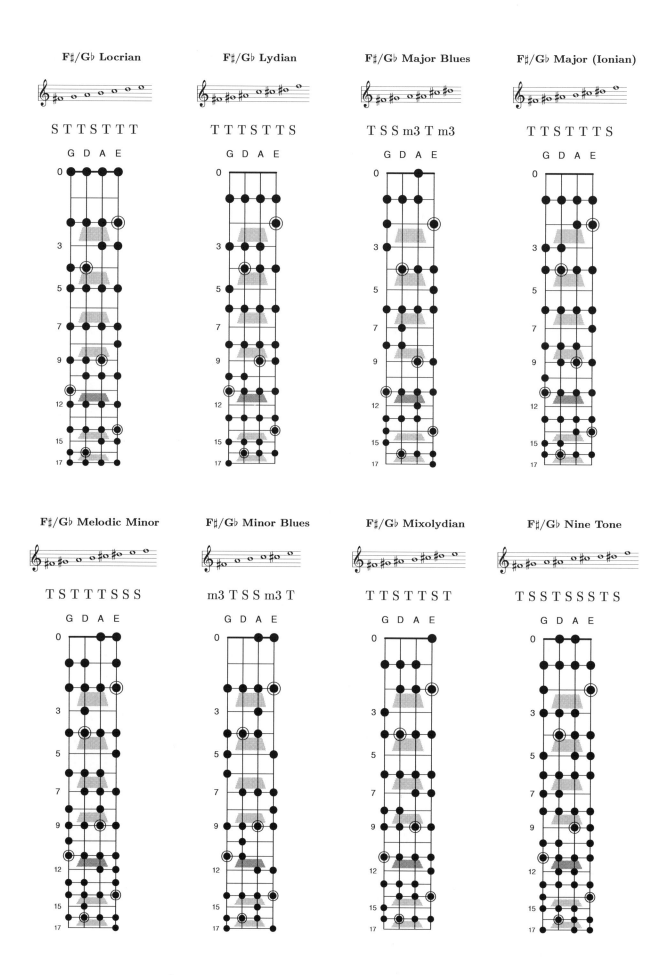

42

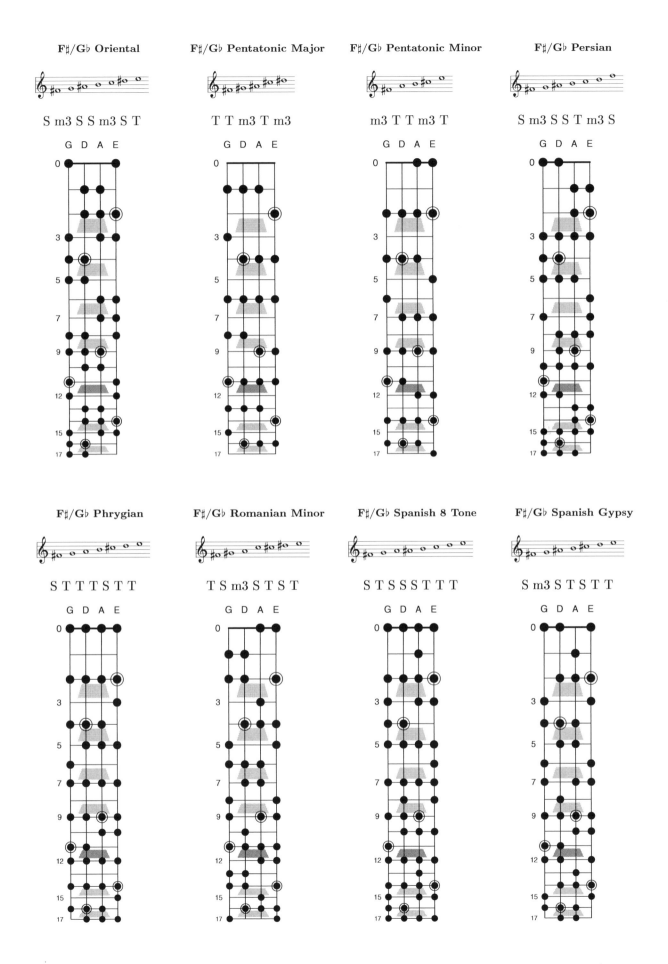

F♯/G♭ Symmetric Dim. 1 **F♯/G♭ Symmetric Dim. 2**

S T S T S T S T   T S T S T S T S

G Aeolian   **G Algerian**   **G Arabic**   **G Bebop Dominant**

T S T T S T T   T S T S S S m3 S   T T S S T T T   T T S T T S S S

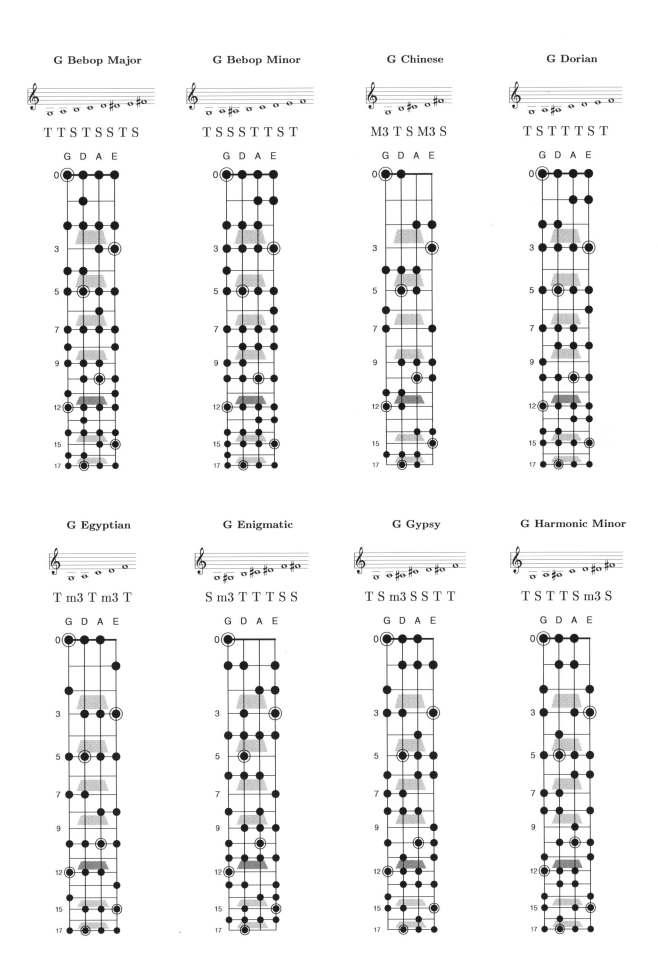

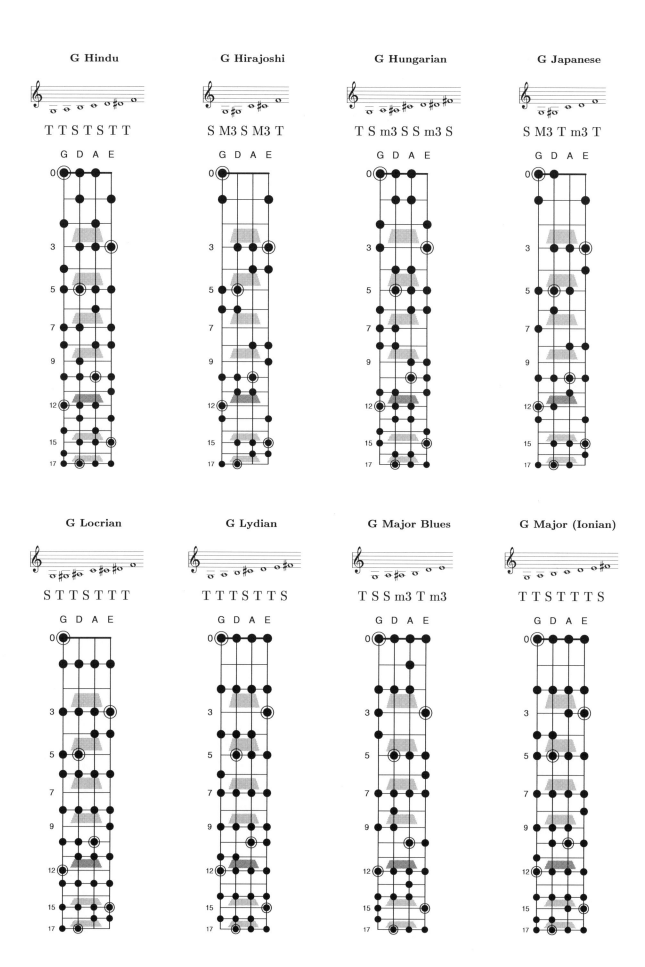

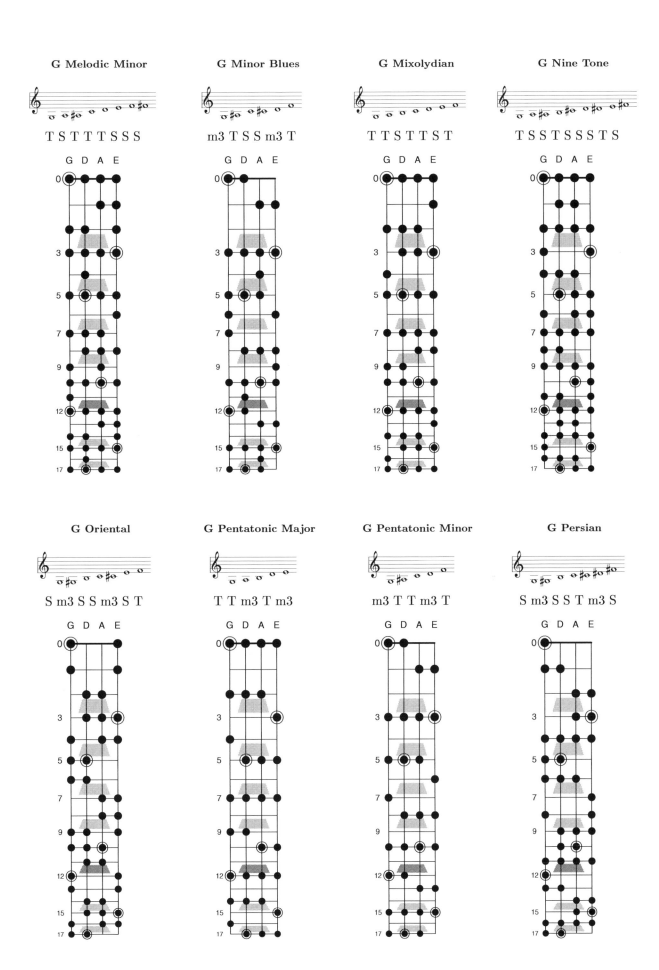

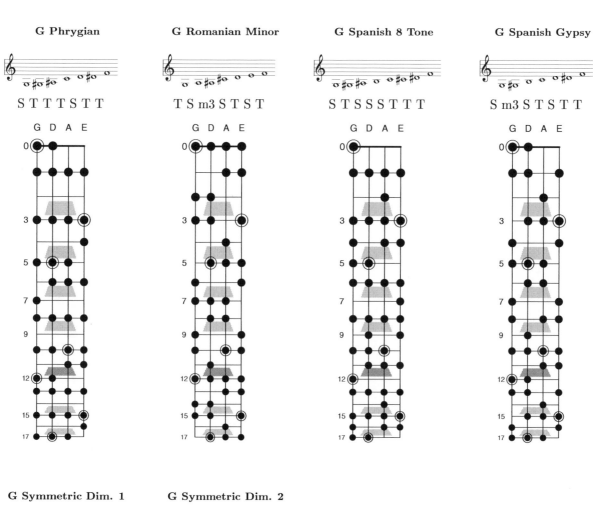

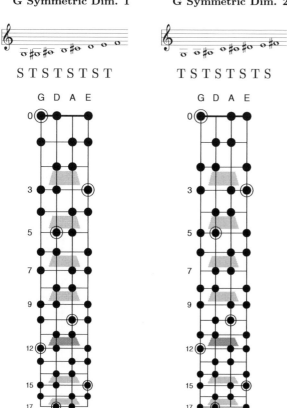

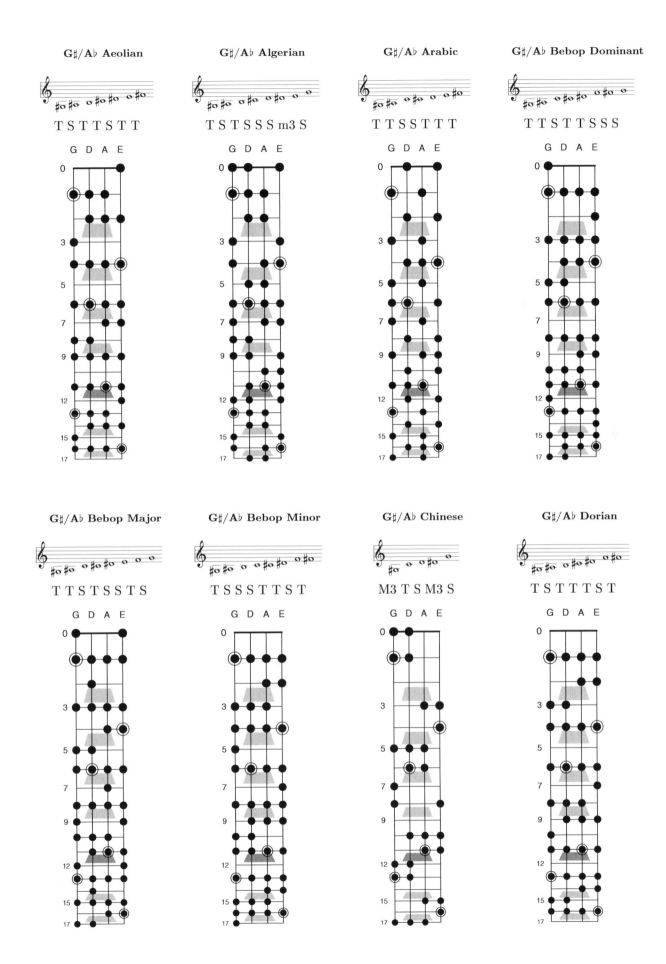

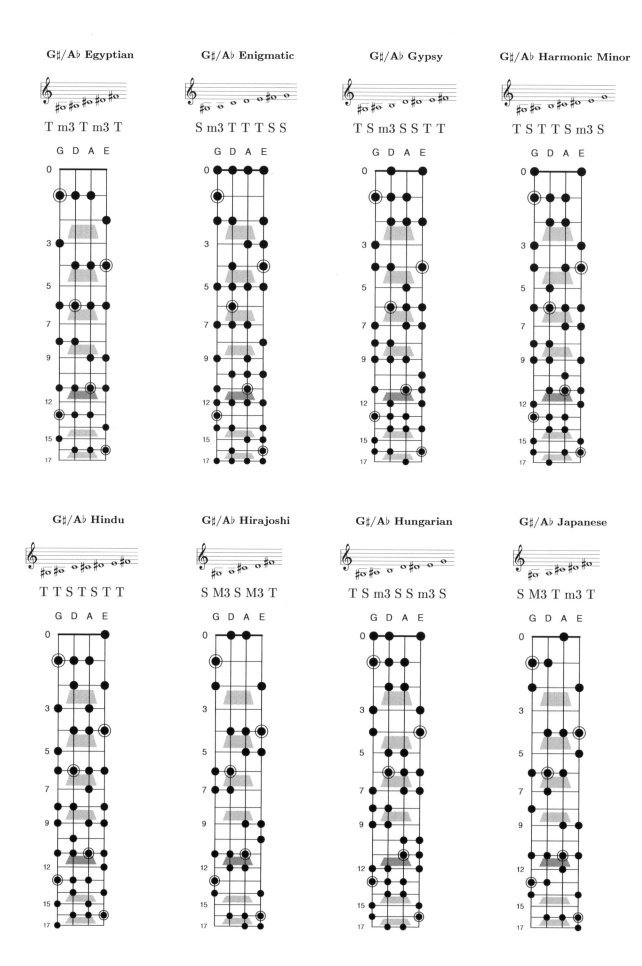

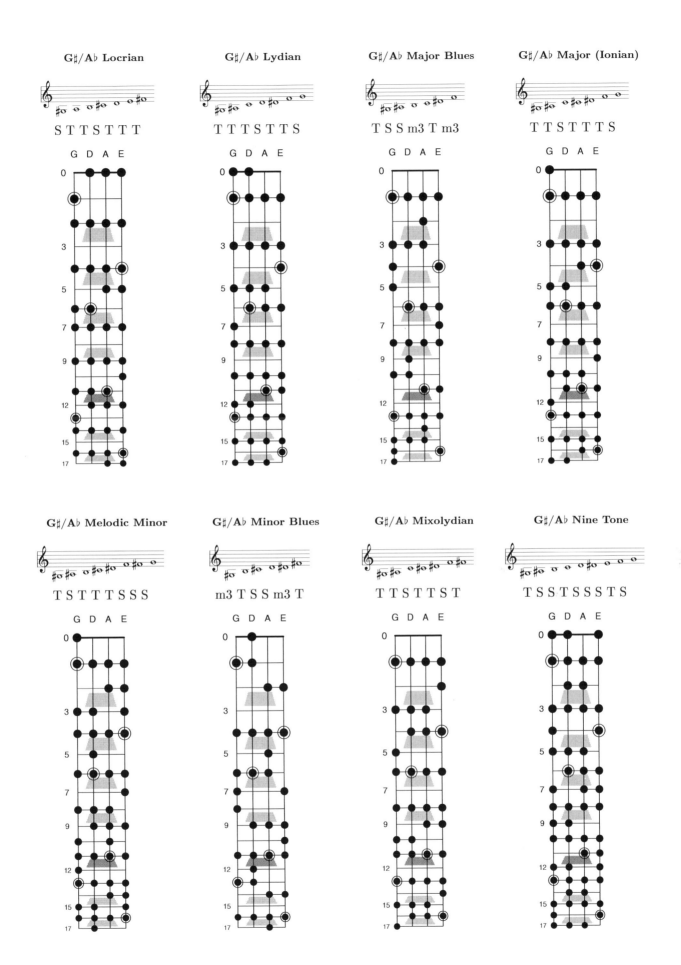

51

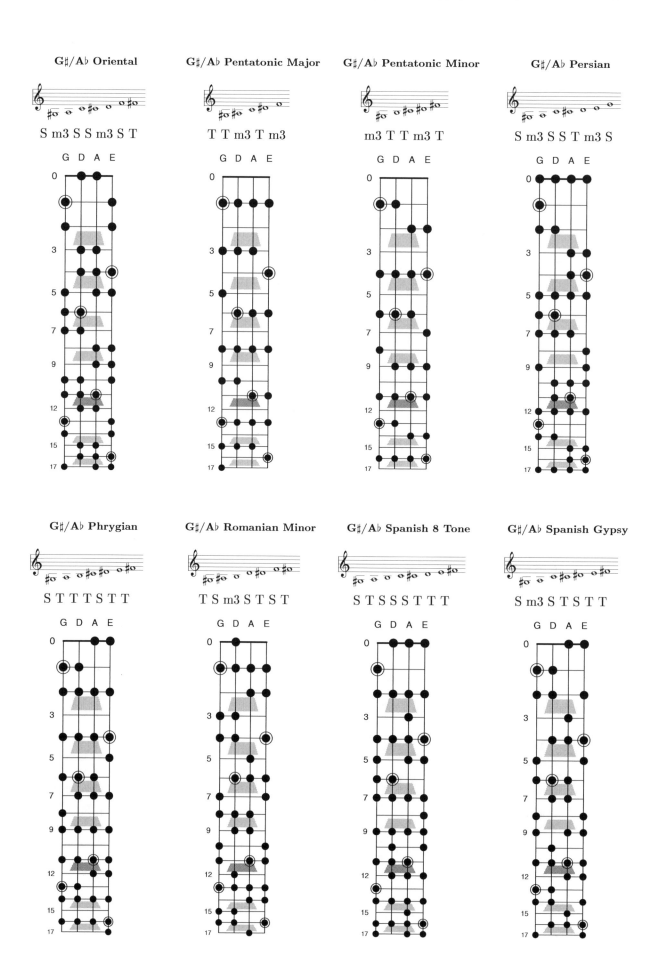

G♯/A♭ Symmetric Dim. 1   G♯/A♭ Symmetric Dim. 2

S T S T S T S T   T S T S T S T S

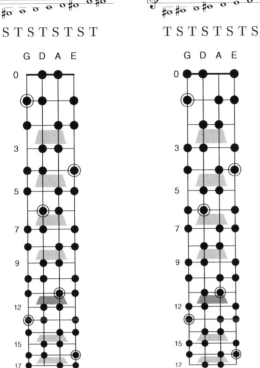

A Aeolian   **A Algerian**   **A Arabic**   **A Bebop Dominant**

T S T T S T T   T S T S S S m3 S   T T S S T T T   T T S T T S S S

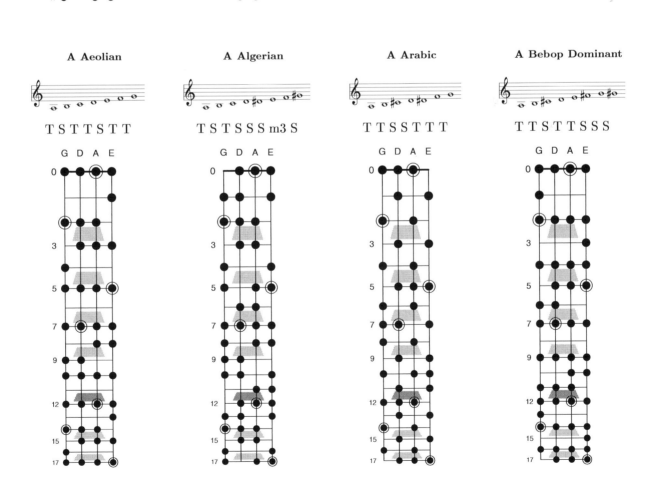

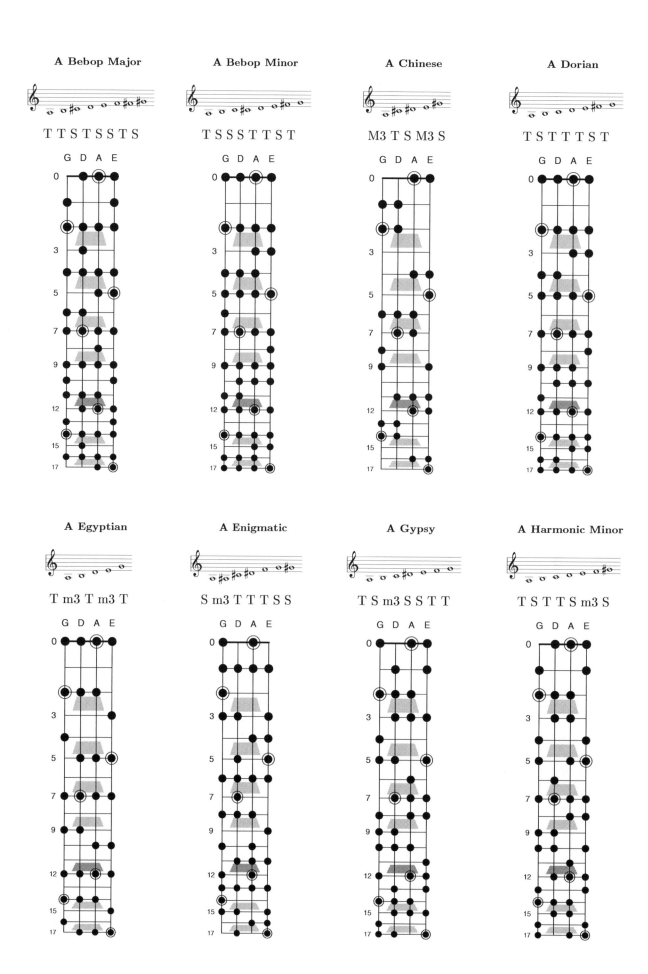

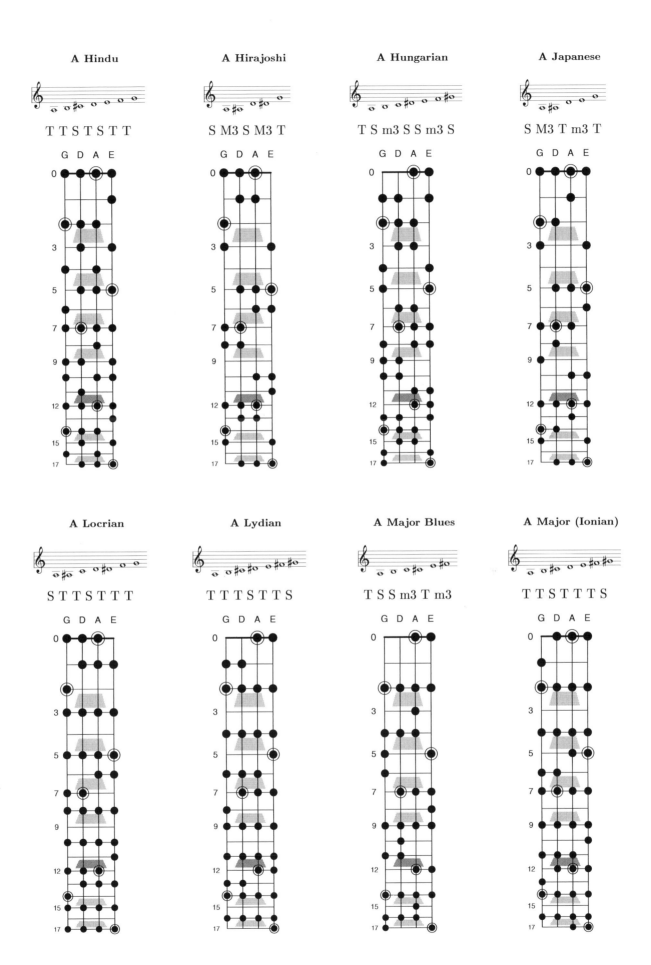

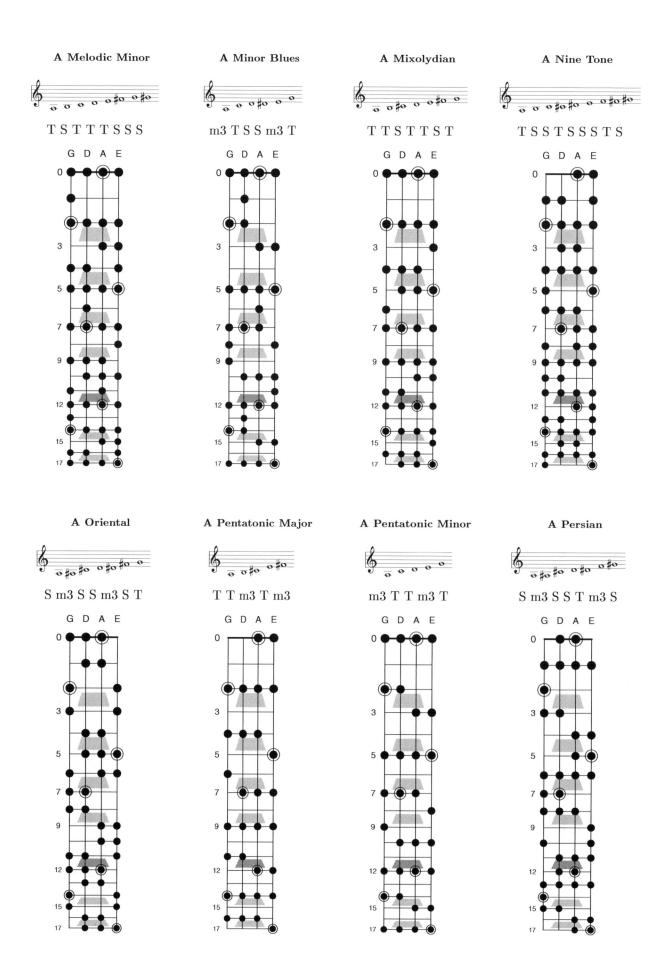

56

A Phrygian

S T T T S T T

A Romanian Minor

T S m3 S T S T

A Spanish 8 Tone

S T S S S T T T

A Spanish Gypsy

S m3 S T S T T

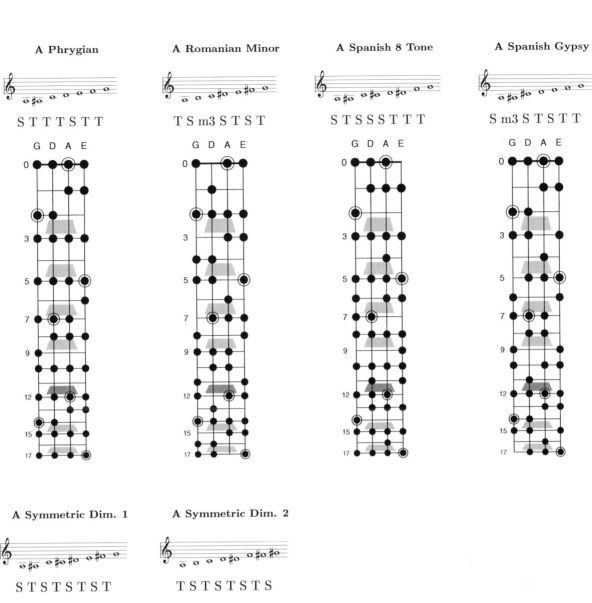

A Symmetric Dim. 1

S T S T S T S T

A Symmetric Dim. 2

T S T S T S T S

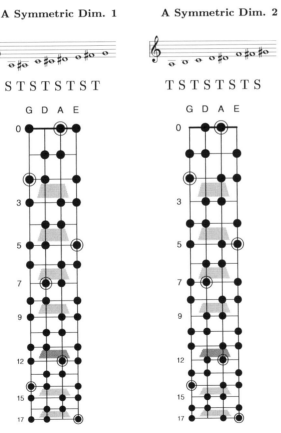

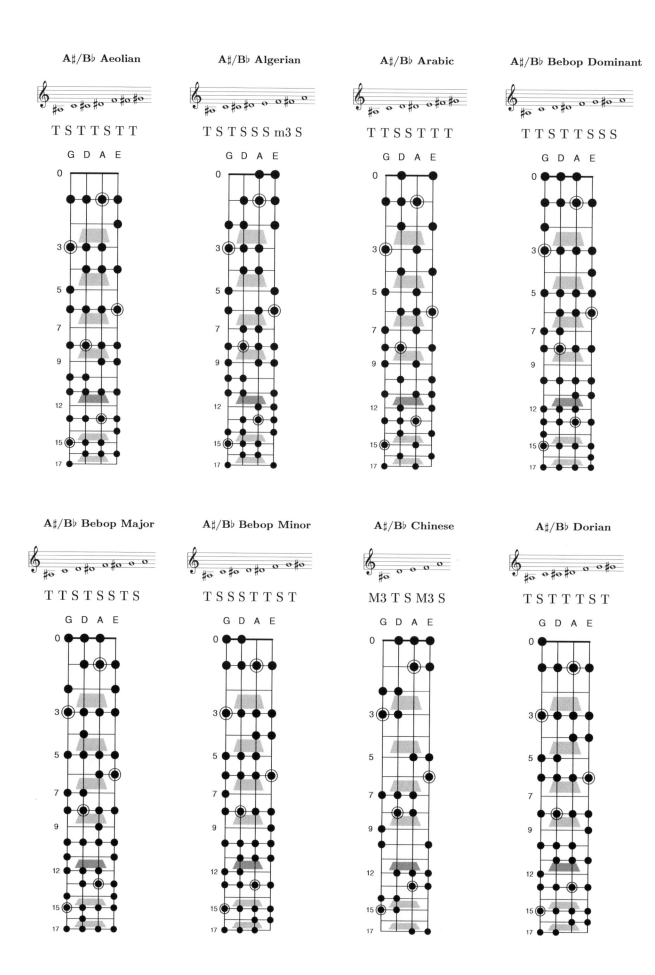

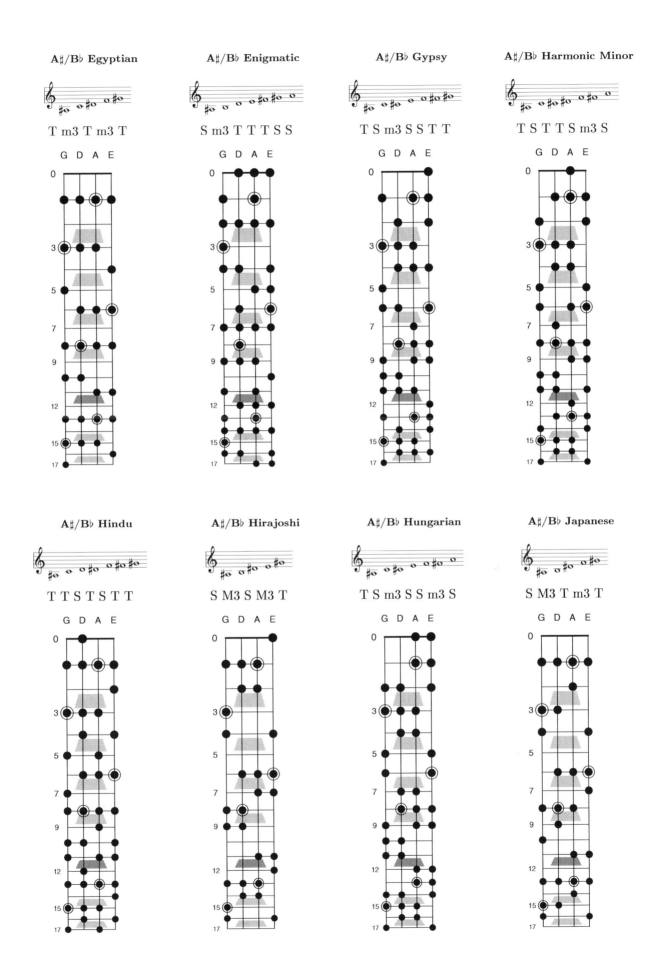

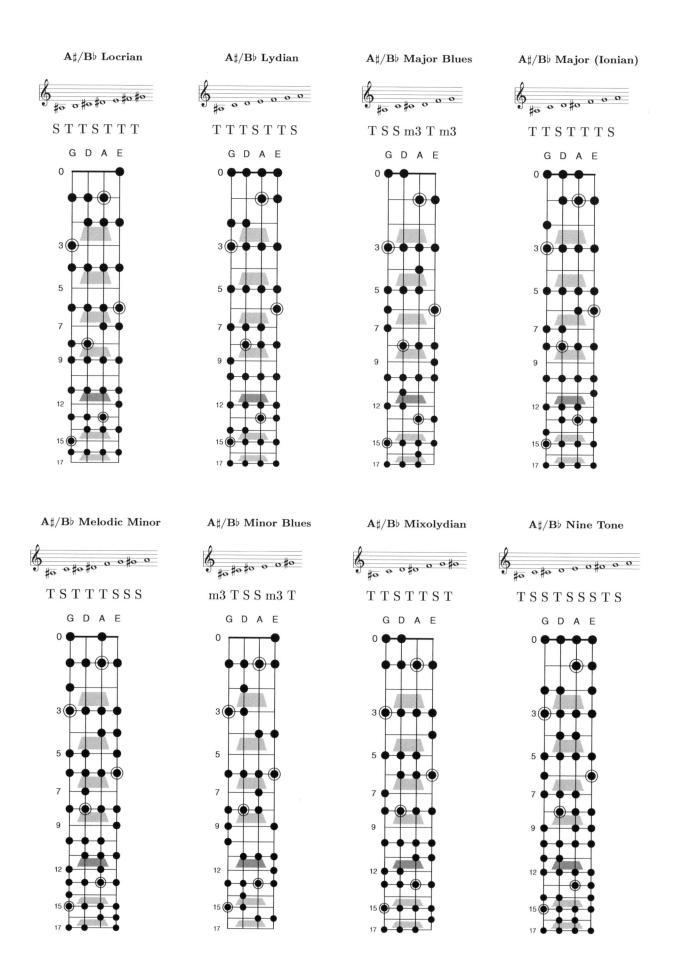

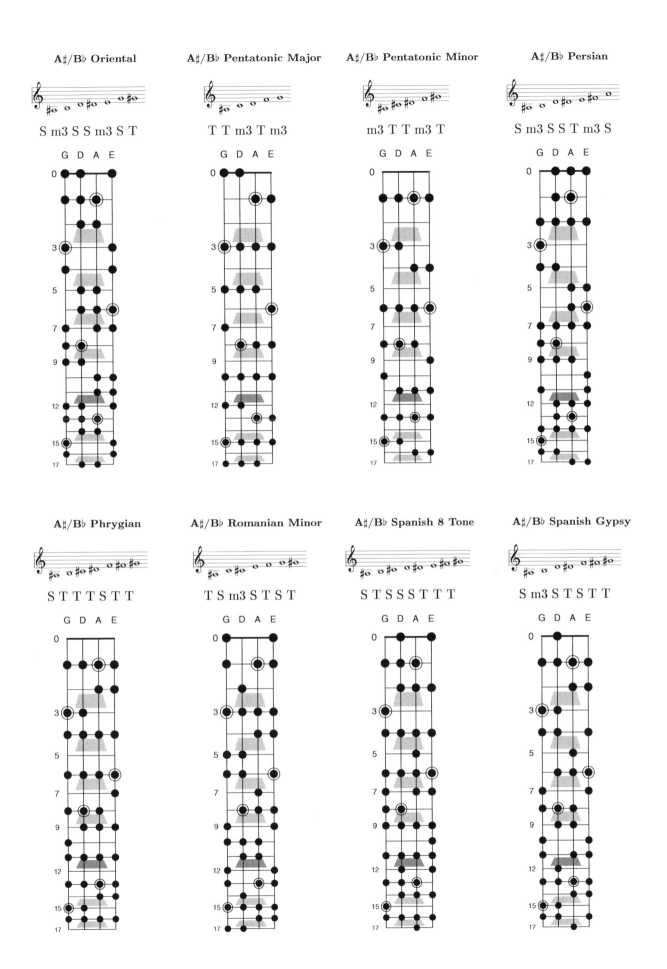

61

A♯/B♭ Symmetric Dim. 1   **A♯/B♭ Symmetric Dim. 2**

S T S T S T S T   T S T S T S T S

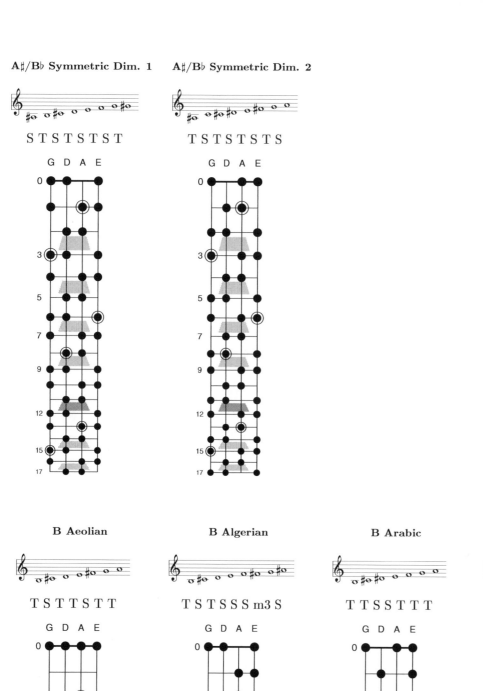

B Aeolian   **B Algerian**   **B Arabic**   **B Bebop Dominant**

T S T T S T T   T S T S S S m3 S   T T S S T T T   T T S T T S S

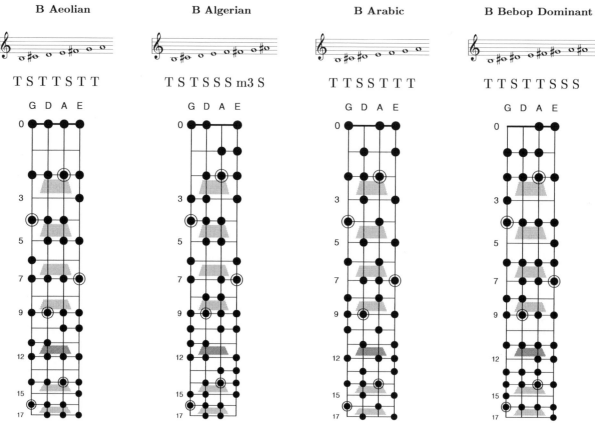

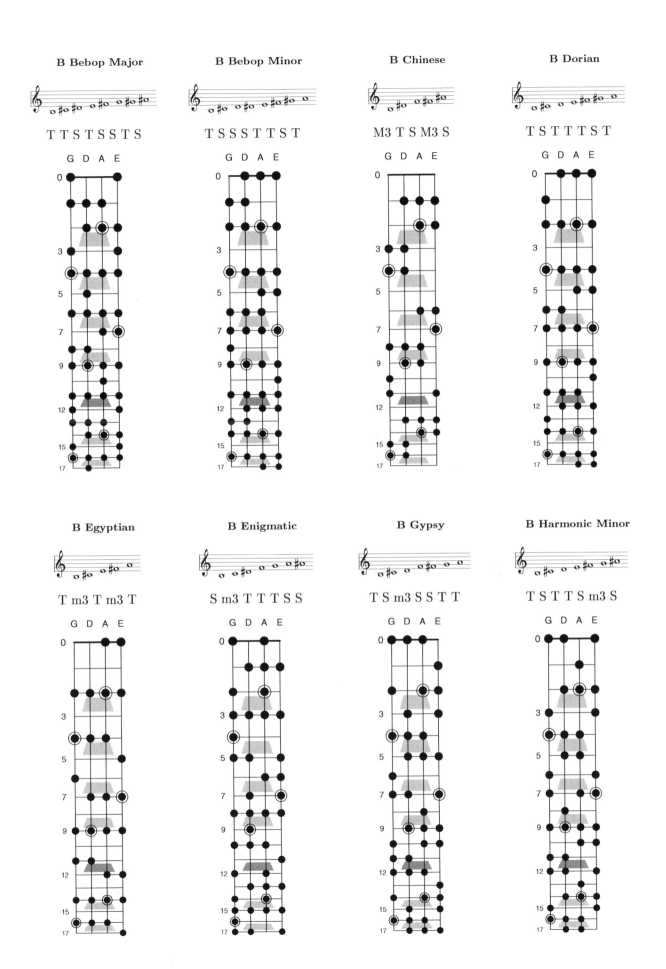

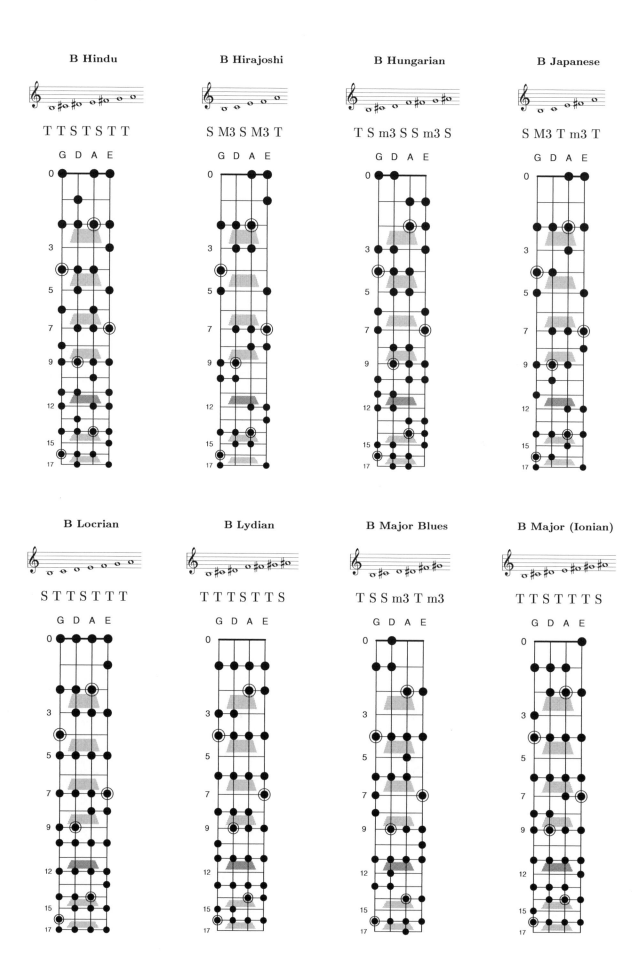

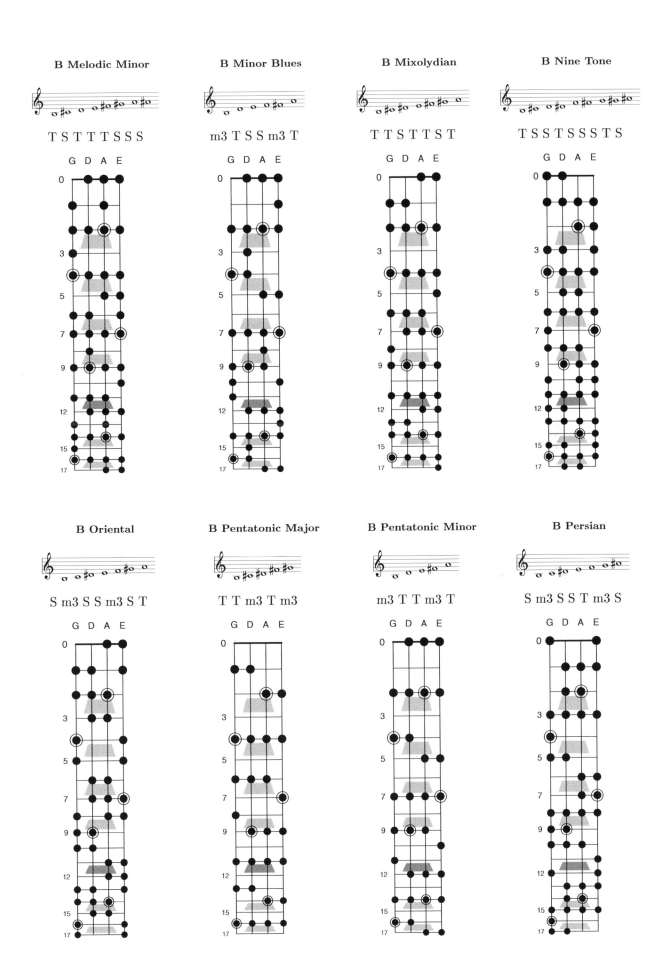

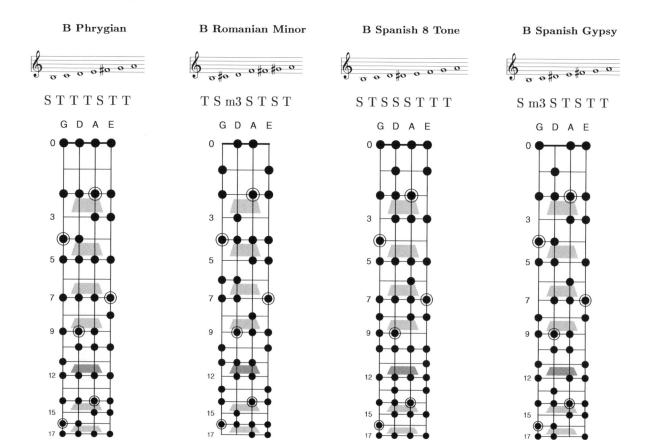

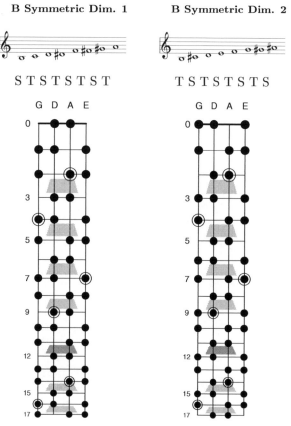

Movable 'Box' Scale Patterns

Aeolian

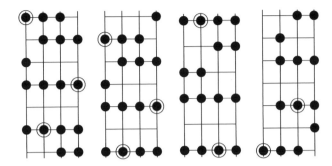

Algerian

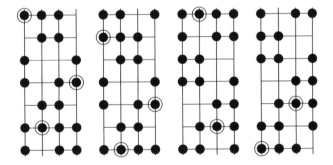

Arabic

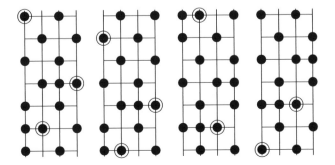

Bebop Dominant

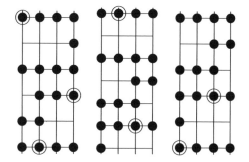

Bebop Major

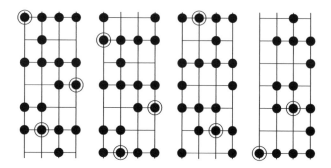

Bebop Minor

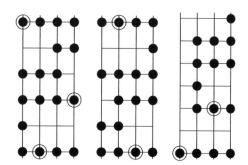

Chinese

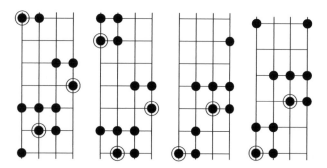

Dorian

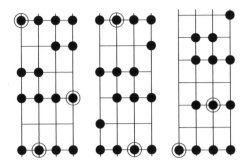

Egyptian

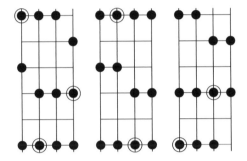

Enigmatic

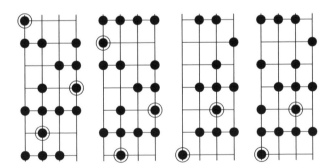

Gypsy

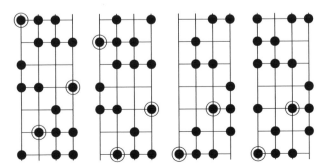

Harmonic Minor

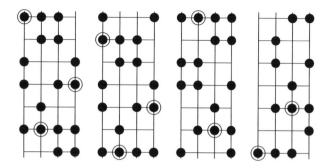

Hindu

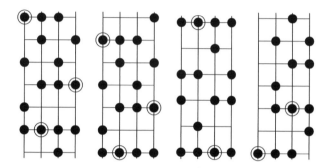

Hirajoshi

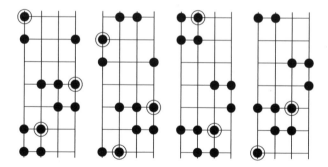

Hungarian

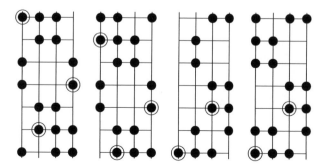

Japanese

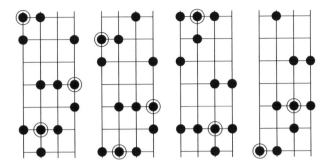

Locrian

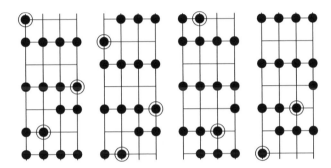

Lydian

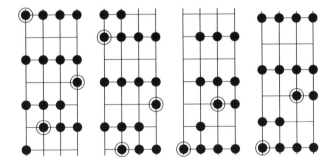

Major Blues

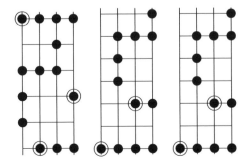

Major (Ionian)

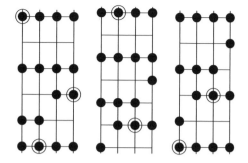

Melodic Minor

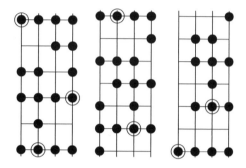

Minor Blues

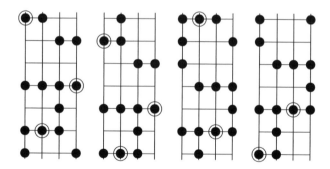

Mixolydian

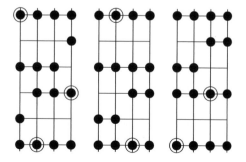

Nine Tone

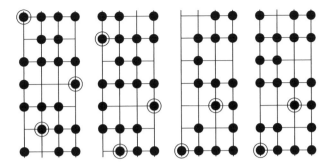

Oriental

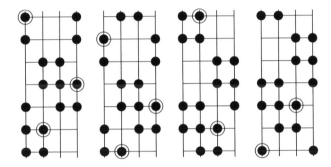

Pentatonic Major

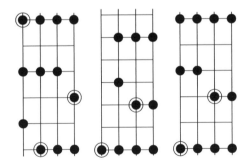

Pentatonic Minor

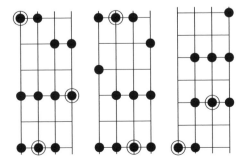

Persian

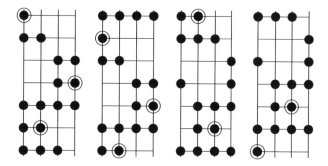

Phrygian

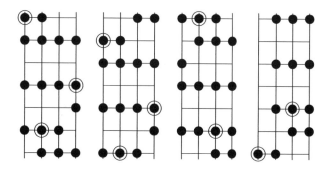

Romanian Minor

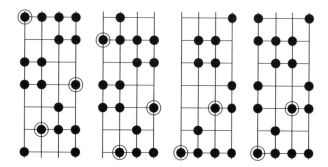

Spanish 8 Tone

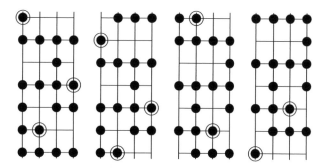

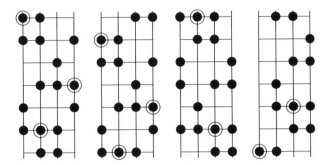

Symmetric Dim. 1

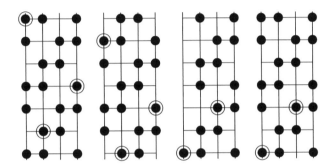

Symmetric Dim. 2

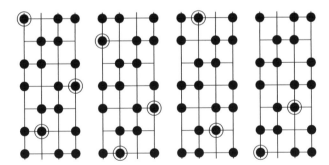

Made in the USA
Middletown, DE
09 May 2023